BECOMING LUCID

Self-Awareness in Sleeping & Waking Life

Hypnotic Practice in Lucidity & Dreams

•

Lincoln Stoller, PhD, CHt

MindStrengthBalance.com

First Edition.
Published 2019 by Mind Strength Balance
Victoria, British Columbia, Canada
https://www.mindstrengthbalance.com

Copyright © 2019 Lincoln Stoller, All rights reserved.
Except for brief excepts in reviews, no part of this book may be reproduced in any form, or by any means, electronic or mechanical, including photocopying, recording, or by any information storage and retrieval system, without the written permission of the publisher.

Stoller, Lincoln, 1956- author.
becoming lucid : self-awareness in sleeping & waking life / Lincoln Stoller.
ISBN 978-1-7752880-8-4 (mobi) | ISBN 978-1-7752880-7-7 (epub)
ISBN 978-1-7752880-5-3 (paper) | ISBN 978-1-7752880-6-0 (hard cover)
ISBN 978-1-7752880-9-1 (audio)
Subjects: LCSH: Awareness. | Dreams. | Mental suggestion. | Sleep.

Cover Photo: Rüştü Bozkuş

Praise for
Becoming Lucid

In this fascinating look inwards, Lincoln Stoller takes the de facto *approach to lucid dreaming and turns it on its head. Rather than yet another guide book, this work represents a paradigm shift to an entirely new mode of thinking. A meaningful and deeply introspective addition to any dreamers bookshelf.*

—**Chris Hammond**, Chief Lucidity Officer at www.world-of-lucid-dreaming.com

~

Delightful! **Becoming Lucid** *fills a huge gap in the lucid literature by developing lucid dreams alongside classic methods of consciousness exploration. Dr. Stoller's altogether rational perspective still leaves room for the mystery and majesty of the unconscious. Hypnosis audio files in each chapter are a most delightful addition. A must for all serious explorers of consciousness.*

—**Ryan Hurd**, author of *Sleep Paralysis*, and *Lucid Immersion Guidebook*. Editor of *Lucid Dreaming: New Perspectives on Consciousness in Sleep*.

~

Not just about dreams, and not just a book. **Becoming Lucid** *links awareness of dreaming and awareness of waking in a practical exploration of your consciousness—and something deeper. It's about being awake to your life, with step-by-step instructions. I recommend this for everyone interested in lucid dreaming and raising their consciousness.*

—**Howard Rheingold**, author of *Excursions to the Far Side of the Mind*, and *Tools for Thought: The History and Future of Mind-Expanding Technology*. Co-author of *Exploring the World of Lucid Dreaming*.

Table of Contents

Acknowledgment...vii
Prologue...1
1 Introduction..3
    Lucidity   3
    State   4
    Perception   7
    Awareness   9
    Who You Are   11
    HYPNOTIC SESSION 1: Remember Dreams   12
2 Having Dreams..19
    Dreams   19
    Anxiety   21
    Ego   21
    Awareness   23
    Clarity   25
    Collaboration   26
    Guidance   27
    HYPNOTIC SESSION 2: Magic Hands   28
3 Finding Meaning..35
    Interpretation: Assembling the Parts   36
        Symbols   37
        Fractals   39
        Active Imagination   42
    Holism   43
    Superposition   45
    Understanding   49
    HYPNOTIC SESSION 3: Tapestry   51
4 Being Lucid..65

Sleep States and Frames of Mind	65
Stage 1	67
Stage 2	68
Stage 3	69
REM Sleep	70
Reality-Checks	70
Awareness	72
Presence: experience, opportunity	72
Reality-Check	74
Reflection: thinking, creation of opportunity	74
Reality-Check	75
Detachment: self-exploration, creation of thinking	76
Reality-Check	78
Intention: opportunity, creation of experience	79
Reality-Check	80
Metacognitive Illusions	80
Pre-lucidity Example: Connecting with the Dream	83
Pre-lucidity Exercise:	
Weaving the Subconscious into the Conscious	84
HYPNOTIC SESSION 4: Mindscape	87
5 Waking Lucidity	**95**
Waking Practice	97
Exercises	97
HYPNOTIC SESSION 5: Being Awake	99
6 Hypnagogic Lucidity	**107**
Hypnagogic Practice	108
Exercises	108
HYPNOTIC SESSION 6: Illuminations	111
7 Dreaming Lucidity	**117**
Dreaming Practice	119
Exercises	120

HYPNOTIC SESSION 7: Stepping Off	122
8 Hypnopompic Lucidity...	131
Hypnopompic Practice	133
Exercises	133
HYPNOTIC SESSION 8: Crossroads	137
9 Beyond Lucidity...	143
Perception	143
Memory	144
States	146
Works	148
Lucidity	148
Theory of Dreams	149
Utility	150
Beyond Dreaming	152
Beyond Lucidity	153
Exercises	154
HYPNOTIC SESSION 9: Welcome to The End	158
Postscript...	169
References...	170
About the Author...	172

with money. An angry person remains angry, a happy person happy, depending on the stability of their state. If you strive to make a lot of money because you need more money, then even when you succeed you still need more money. Tunnel vision affects where you look and determines what you see.

Changes of state are usually changed by feelings in the normal course of events. Feelings so much define our state that I assert we feel, therefore we are. When feeling secure nothing shakes you; when feeling scared everything shakes you. Your feelings more determine what you perceive, than the other way around. Perception is not a passive act, even when you think it is, which is most of the time. Thinking doesn't have much to do with being.

Awareness

This brings us to awareness. How aware are you of the world around you? How aware are you of your perception? Awareness is the responsibility you take for your perception.

If you do not take responsibility for what you perceive in the waking world, then you will not do so in the non-waking world. This is why both worlds seem so real. We typically take both of them as absolutes, in and of themselves, from the start. In short, we exert little awareness in either. The first lesson of lucid dreaming, perhaps ironically, is that you're not controlling your reality anywhere!

And so, we return to state. You control your state by being aware, which means examining and actively engaging in your perception. It is not, as you might think, a process of lifting yourself up by your bootstraps. It is simply and carefully examining your bootstraps, and whatever is attached to them. It involves looking into, and looking out of alternatives.

Introduction

The water is at rest in the unmoving bucket, so we call that "the resting state." It takes effort to get the bucket spinning, and once spinning it will keep spinning, and we call that "the excited state." These states look and behave differently, and you can do different things with them. You can form a bucket brigade with buckets at rest and thereby move water. You can contrive machines with spinning buckets that will send the spinning energy elsewhere. From different states, different relationships emerge.

When you're depressed you see, sense, and act one way; when angry another. Focus on American Politics over coffee, but not during orgasm. And within these various states of mind different world views take form, and different understandings emerge. Depending on what state you have been in, you will be in a different state when you return to "normal."

Once set spinning you will stay spinning, like the bucket; because we're talking about mind, the "spinning" takes place in your imagination. Our state of mind is not what we perceive, rather, it is the sum total of what we have, are now, and will perceive. Which is to say, your state determines the thoughts and feelings you remember, experience, and imagine. And from that state, new states emerge that were otherwise inaccessible.

Moving from despair to elation requires something in between. The states of mind you aspire to, require other states as steps to getting there. As you change your state, you engage the feedback between being and perceiving. In this, you take an active role in what you perceive. You do this even in what we call "the waking world."

Changes in state of mind are rarely the result of changes in what you perceive, as what you perceive is generated from the state. That is to say, normal events do not change your state of mind. Give money to a homeless person and they become a homeless person

Acknowledgment

No one enlightens another; some higher force does. When my sight is changed and—like Polyphemus—I exclaim, "No-one has enlightened me!" no one understands.

Prologue

Most self-help books don't have a plot, but this one does. The search for lucidity is a mystery that unfolds as we search for clues. Unlike a novel, our plot does not conclude. Or, you might say, it concludes in the way Moby Dick concludes: we find the White Whale but cannot contain it.

Finding lucidity is the first step, just a doorway. Once you gain lucidity, the real question is what are you now lucid of? Like the White Whale, once we obtain lucidity, we must leave behind the skills that got us there in order to go further.

The quest for lucidity is a journey across a desert of awareness. We learn to track, navigate, and commit ourselves. We develop our skills with the exercises in this book and travel to the limits of our self-control and self-awareness. When we finally become lucid—whatever that means to each of us—we reach the eye of a needle. At that point the path takes a 90-degree turn… up!

If you've been searching for lucidity, this will not be news to you. It takes a good deal of work and study to reach that point where work and study no longer serve us; a point where every answer you get multiplies your questions in ever greater numbers. We aim to go as far as we can on the path to lucidity, and then to learn the nature of what lies beyond. Let's see if we can get there!

Lincoln Stoller, 2019

www.mindstrengthbalance.com and www.mindstrengthbooks.com.
Follow @LincolnStoller and #BecomingLucid

Note to the Reader

Each chapter in this book ends with a hypnotic session presenting the material in a manner that engages your emotions and detaches you from your senses. However, if you are reading this, then you may not benefit from these sessions since the act of reading contains you within a nonemotional, verbal state of mind. To gain the most benefit from these sessions, they should be read to you.

To make this possible for readers of the text, at the start of each session, I have included a link to folder on the internet that contains MP3 sound files which you can download. In this folder there is a sound file for each hypnotic session, and you may listen to these files at your convenience. They may put you to sleep but, as long as it is a light sleep, you will hear and appreciate them.

The URL for this folder is:

https://www.mindstrengthbalance.com/becoming-lucid-audio/

— CAUTION —

Do not listen to these audio files while driving a car, operating machinery, or doing anything that requires your attention!

1 Introduction

"... becoming aware is infinitely fertile."
— Johann Wolfgang von Goethe (1749—1842)

Where other books on lucid dreaming focus on the dreaming, this book focuses on becoming lucid in both the sleeping and waking state. Dreams can offer an easier path to lucidity because of the contrast between dreaming and lucidity: you think you're not lucid in normal dreams, so you understand what you're trying to accomplish. In truth, we don't know what lucid means, we don't really know the final goal. That doesn't matter too much, as it still gives us a path to follow. The process of learning to lucid dream is a heuristic, like this book is a heuristic: it's a means to an end, a means for exploring consciousness.

Lucidity

Clear understanding is based on clear definitions, which discussions on lucid dreaming lack. Try as I might, I find no clear definition of lucidity. But in order to get started, here are two possibilities.

Conventional dream lucidity refers to becoming aware that you're dreaming while you're dreaming. This definition fails because everything we experience resides in our imagination; reality itself is a dream-form. "I am dreaming," is a dream statement which does not necessarily change anything, though it might.

A better definition of lucidity is a dream situation where the results of your actions are consistent with your expectations. According to this definition, you are lucid when you want something to happen, you act to make it happen, and it happens. You feel you're in control even if, in retrospect, your control is minimal to none.

When the world behaves according to your expectations you can successfully interact with it: you have a degree of identity, authority, and control. In contrast, if the world fails to react in ways you expect then you're lost and you cannot understand it. A well-behaved world strengthens your assumptions; a misbehaving world challenges them.

The primary distinction between lucid and nonlucid dreams is that lucidity gives you the impression that your perceptions make sense and you can predict the results of your actions. We call this experience "reality." In contrast, the normal dream paradigm is that our actions are not reasoned, and their results are not reasonable.

These definitions are incomplete. We seem to be meaning more than either of them describe. What we really seem to mean by dream lucidity is being fully awake when we're fully asleep, which is an oxymoron. Therefore I back off from defining lucidity as a concept, and I approach it as a state.

State

See lucidity as a state of mind. States of mind are poorly understood. Spend time with me now to consider the notion of state, and the feeling of being in a state. We'll use some ideas from science, though this is somewhat self-defeating. Science is objective, and states are not. You can only go so far when applying the wrong tool for the job. States of mind are the result of dynamic interactions between many systems; states emerge to float above the systems of which they're composed, like the "intelligence" of a computer, which cannot be found anywhere in its parts.

Think of the force that causes water to climb the walls of a spinning bucket. The force is not in the water, it's not in the bucket, and it's not in the action of turning itself. Examine each separately and you'll never understand why the water rises out of the spinning bucket, which only happens when all the elements are combined and set in motion. To explain this, we use terms like inertia and momentum, but we don't know where they come from. So it is with states of mind: they do not reside in the parts, the forces, or the mixtures of them, but rather in them all combined and interacting.

We want to appreciate the range and depth of states. You are not a spinning bucket of water, nor are you a complicated biological machine, because neither concept contains the emergent qualities we're looking for. Consider the biological model so often taken for granted.

It is said your brain is the domicile of your mind, so as to imply your state of mind lies within it. Your brain is made of nerves of special types and properties, sustained by known chemical and metabolic processes: nutrition, synaptic communication, membranes, chemical production, and cellular growth. Our description of these processes are based on opposites, as boundaries are the basis of measurement: sizes, concentrations, thresholds, and components. From this derives the notion of the brain as a computer, and the mind as software.

But the brain's behavior is only weakly described in these terms. For the most part, the brain's activity is collective, and what the ensemble displays is suspiciously unseen in the behavior of its parts. Yes, nerves charge, and synapses fire, but most nerves, most of the time, in the aware, awake, and active brain, are measurably silent. Yes, it is true that low level, collective, electrical excitation ruffles through the brain, like the wind through the trees, but we cannot pinpoint where this "wind" is coming from.

If you go inside of a brain cell and listen to what's coming and going through its cytoplasm, then you'll hear all sorts of "things" that are not evident, or audible outside each cell, or between them. None of this is digital, only a small portion of it involves chemical reactions, as most of it involves the electrical transport of chemicals, the rotation of molecules, and the rearrangement of parts... like water climbing up the side of a bucket.

It has become possible to see smaller structures, and sub-microscopic processes. Within each cell exist other cell-like things. Components that have their own membrane, metabolism, autonomy, and control. It seems that each cell—and not just nerve cells but all cells—have microtubule structures within which are smaller structures that change state, store information, and control the processes of the cell.

The amount of information stored in the microtubules of each cell approximates the amount of information that the brain was expected to store through the interaction of cells within it. Now it seems the "ghost" of the mind within the brain, has an equally large number of ghosts of potentially equally large minds within them.

A number of these structures, genes in particular but not exclusively, do not die with the cell, or even with the organism. Rather, they are passed roughly intact from parent cell to child cell and from human parents to their children. If elements of mind exist in these structures—and it's clear that some attitudes and behaviors

Becoming Lucid

are inherited—then not only can't we locate the mind in space, but we can't locate it in time, either. That is to say, the organism may die, but some parts of what we consider "mind" do not.

Finding where the mind resides is an aspect of what's called "the hard problem." It's fair to argue that we know next to nothing about it. I believe some of the predictions we hear about finally understanding the mind—such as the idea of "the singularity," whereupon the brain will finally and faithfully be recreated in silicon—are the last, dying gasps of the naïve idea that we'll be able to understand our minds by breaking them down into their smallest component pieces.

I mention this only to enlarge your notion of state. Just as we do not know where the mind is, we do not know where the state is. There are some things we're aware of, and some things we can measure, and there are some things which you will become aware of, and by that way understand better. Which brings us to the issue of perception.

Perception

To say that our state of mind is what we perceive it to be, may seem to be stating the obvious, but it's not obvious, and it's not true. The problem lies in the words "perceive" and "to be," and the problem is that you can't have one without the other. They are two aspects of the same thing, so one can't define the other. It is a tautology, like saying "I am me;" a tautology explains nothing.

If the Cartesian mindset says, "I think therefore I am," then what about our feelings and perceptions? And if your state of mind changes, where has the "thinking" gone that previously defined you? These are old arguments that track mud into the house. Let's return to the spinning bucket.

Introduction

You have the potential to become more aware and involved in your perceptions. It is normal to think of perception and reception as identical, as befits the assumption that you perceive what is there. This is untrue at four levels to start with.

Perceptions are composed of engagement, reception, processing, and interpretation. Engagement is orienting; being aware of your situation. Reception is receiving sensation; being aware of your focus. Processing is recognizing that you're recognizing; being aware of how you're filtering information. Interpretation is a conscious, unconscious, or subconscious process that leads to taking action. The four components of perception occur in sequence and, in themselves, form one of the legs on which lucidity stands.

Throughout this book we distinguish unconscious actions of habit from subconscious actions of judgement. You do unconsciously what you once were, and are still programmed to do. You're acting out of reflex. You act subconsciously when you base your actions on intuition, emotion, or instinct. Some analysis may occur, but this analysis is just a glue connecting feelings with action.

Perception and sensation occur simultaneously and most sensations are not perceived, they're handled unconsciously. Few of our senses are well developed, oriented, engaged, or their results recognized. Their list consists of the physical and subtle senses. We all have experience developing our senses, and any sense we have can be improved.

The physical senses are the familiar five: taste, smell, touch, sight, and hearing, plus the less familiar four: proprioception (sense of movement), balance (orientation in space), temperature, and pain. To this we may add seven subtle senses: telepathic, clairsentient (visual, auditory, sensory), mystic, contemplative, intuitive, psychic, and energetic.

Becoming Lucid

You may say the subtle senses are not real, or that you don't have them, but you don't know. If they exist, you have them. You may object, and say you only signed up to wake up in your dreams. That's a limitation, get over it! We're here to make real what is now potential. Through the practices in this book, you will become more aware of your senses.

Who You Are

Fear and need keep us limited to what we have. Fear and need also motivate us to reach for what we don't. And when that happens, fear turns into a kind of lust, and the burning sense of need becomes sweet with opportunity.

This is a change you can make, and it will happen more often, and more quickly, if you see your fear as tempter or temptress. See your need as a need to grow into your power. Turn and focus on the scent of power. Do not take who you are for granted.

"They say we only use a fraction of our brain's true potential. Now that's when we're awake. When we're asleep, we can do almost anything."

— Cobb, from the movie *Inception*.

Hypnotic Session 1

Remember Dreams audio file at:
https://www.mindstrengthbalance.com/becoming-lucid-audio/

Remember Dreams

In this exercise, deeply immerse yourself in the image of what you're doing. You need to see yourself as if you were looking at yourself, and feel as if you were remembering, and sense—as much as you can—in your body and in your mind, that you are present in the experience that you are re-creating. So that when you finish this, and you think back on it, you can't remember if you were imagining that you were thinking these things, or if you were thinking them and you're remembering it. This is the essential aspect of hypnosis, in this case self-hypnosis: you must really put yourself in the place you want to go.

This session starts like all sessions, with relaxation, because relaxation means release, and what you want to release is your sense of difference, presence, separateness, and ultimately time. Begin by relaxing in your position, be it a chair, a bed, a couch—it can really be anywhere. It pays to be able to release even the tension that holds you up, but you don't have to. As long as you're comfortable, you can sit erect and still.

Put your hands on your lap, on the table, or on the arms of the chair. Anywhere you can forget about them. And forget about your feet, and be supported as much as you can, without moving or straining a muscle, and move down through your body as if you were a scanner, passing through your body like a cross section, releasing and dissolving, and unfastening your connection with each sense, muscle, and tissue, as you go.

Start at the top of your head. Take a breath, hold it for a moment, and as you let it out feel relaxation spread over the top of your scalp, so when your breath is exhaled your scalp is relaxed. And with each breath, move down your body; starting with your head and your face. With the exhale relax, like a wave moving down your cheeks, ears, over your nose, past your chin, inhaling again, and exhaling all the sensation out of your shoulders, arms, into the center of your chest. Imaging yourself as thinner, and less substantial. Imagine the inhale coming in through all your skin, and the exhale pouring out through holes all over your body. Inhale... hold it... exhale.

With each breath, and each scan, imagine becoming more relaxed, imagine yourself dissolving, becoming lighter. Images like ballast being dropped from a balloon, or warm water, or thoughts floating away, issues being forgotten, voices becoming distant. Let yourself flow with your body's rhythms and sensations, the natural rhythmic ones. Be more present. You might feel the pulse in your hands, and you might let your breath go down, deep into your stomach, and you might feel energy running over the surface of your skin. And if you don't feel it, then imagine you do, because nothing happens in your mind without the help of your imagination.

Maybe you are a musical person, or a sensory person—call those senses in. Listen, feel, see, smell. Be where you want yourself to be: relax and dissolve. Breathe in and hold it, as it fills down through your pelvis, your gut, your seat. Exhale and relax

Introduction

more deeply. Inhale, hold it, and exhale down through your thighs and your knees and your shins. Inhale ... and exhale.

Feel the warmth in your joints, and the warmth in your hands, and in your feet. That's called progressive relaxation, and in addition to releasing tensions it releases irritable sensations and disconnects you from the annoying present process of thinking. You follow my words and think as slowly as I speak, and you hang on each syllable, so that they resound in your head. Your own thoughts pop like bubbles, like popcorn, or a breeze rustling, flocks of birds that come and go, leaving thoughts unfinished in your head.

Now imagine, and sense, that you're lying in your bed about the time you're about to fall asleep. Some people take longer and some people take shorter, but no one is really present at the moment they fall asleep. You know that feeling that happens when you start to get groggy, that feeling when you've started to stop thinking about going to sleep? Sort of like waiting for a movie to start, and it starts, and for a few brief moments you're not thinking about anything.

Put yourself back in that place. Imagine it's dark, imagine it's warm. You're comfortable, and for the moment you've stopped thinking. Not that you tried to, but it just seems that you forgot, you forgot what you were going to think about.

It seems that someone is coming up from behind you, in your mind, and you know who it is, it's your deeper self, relieved that you are finally stepping out, so that like the janitor after the building closes, in your subconscious mind, you can get to work, and start putting things back together.

And in this moment of pause and emptiness, imagine you have one last phrase to speak to yourself, and you're not sure whether it comes from your intention, or from the deeper part of yourself that seems to be rising. And that one last phrase is this: "I will remember my dreams... I will remember my dreams." And you know what you're talking about.

You're talking about the distant morning, when things will be very different. You will be coming up, and you will be feeling different, and the temperature will be different. The rustle of your clothes and sheets will be different. Your sensations will be different, as if there was a kind of internal alarm alerting you to the coming day. It will be different.

In that different moment of the morning time, as you see it now as you're slipping into sleep, you will remember what you dreamt. It might be a little bit... it might not be a long narrative, just a few images and feelings—the things that were tailing away as you woke up.

And it's important to let yourself wake up gently, to give yourself enough sleep, because dreams don't come if you're deprived of sleep—not well, anyway—and the process needs to be gentle, because there are things that go and things that come, and you will watch them.

Sort of like changing the set on a stage: you want to be present enough in the new act to remember what was on the stage in the old act. And you will remember your dreams. This is the phrase that you can see in your mind, hear in your ears, and

Introduction

feel resounding in your body. I will remember my dreams.

What I'd like you to do is to play this tape as you're going to sleep and employ a few other reminders as well. Say to yourself, quite artificially and without any particular suggestion, that you will remember your dreams. Just remind yourself of that. You need to do it at several different levels: the somnambulistic level, the hypnagogic level, the conscious level, the dreamy level, the analytical level.

These levels are like layers of dough. They collectively gain strength, and if they all remind each other that you will remember your dreams, then no one—when you're coming out of sleep and putting yourself back together in the morning—will forget to pick up the thread that will be left upon waking. "You will remember your dreams," is the start of everything here. And it's the start of waking up in more ways than one.

Come back now. Let's walk you back. Let's rise up as if we were filling you up—as if you were an empty glass vessel—and you pour in awakeness as if it was water. It collects in your feet and rises up bubbling, cool, and refreshing, and revitalized, up past your shins, filling your knees, through your legs, into your thighs, into your pelvis, into your seat, up to the small of your back. Up into your stomach, filling you with awareness. Up to your ribs, up to your breast, up to your collar bones, up to your shoulders. Filling up your arms with awareness, presence, crisp, and clear, and clean.

Cleaner than it was before, clearer and more pointed, focused, feeling good, feeling clean, feeling crisp, up through your neck,

Becoming Lucid

into your skull, through your jaw, face, ears. Filling the sockets of your eyes, up to the top of your head. And just like it is when you overfill a bottle: it flows out over the top, cascading down like an aura around your body. And you're back, and you're here, and you're awake, and you're present.

Introduction

2 Having Dreams

> *"Dream content in general is continuous with waking conceptions and emotional preoccupations."*
> — G. William Domhoff (2001). "A New Neurocognitive Theory of Dreams." in *Dreaming*, 11(1)

We remember dreams when it's useful and normally don't because it isn't. Following that logic, this chapter is less about remembering dreams and more about making memorable dreams useful.

Dreams

The *locus coeruleus* is a small area in your brainstem, highly integrated with the rest of your brain, and strongly linked to arousal, vigilance, and attention. Its neurons become more active during stress at which time it releases the stress-activating hormone norepinephrine, which stimulates other parts of the brain. The locus coeruleus is almost completely inactivate during the periods of our most visual, dramatic, and potentially lucid dreams. Nightmares aside, it seems we are designed to be insensitive to stress while dreaming.

What might be more useful about having dreams you don't

remember than having dreams you do? The answer lies in our recollection of dreams and in one of their primary aspects: our sense of powerlessness. Being aware and powerless generates anxiety, and it is that feature, I suggest, that allows dreams to better achieve their purpose of measuring, comparing, arranging, and integrating experience when we are absent. We don't like anxiety, and the exploration of things that make us anxious is better done when our anxious selves are absent, which is when we're in the dream state.

Imagine the anxiety you would feel witnessing a surgical operation on yourself. The sense of risk and helplessness would cause more trauma than good. A dream is a rearrangement of our psychic organs, and it proceeds more expeditiously without our being witness. Forcing dream recollection is akin to barging into the operating room. Most likely, the operation is concluded, deferred, or postponed.

Our efforts at recall or lucidity hardly affect our dreaming, as we're dreaming for most of the night, and exerting our efforts to remember during a small part of it. As such, dream recall hardly invades but a small fraction of our dreams. And when we do remember our dreams, what we recall rarely encompasses more than a few minutes, sometimes no more than an instant. Chemically speaking, the brain chemicals necessary for remembering are in short supply during dreaming.

To better remember our dreams, stop trying to catch them and, instead, come into allegiance with them. Work to create a conscious dream-compatible state. It is the difference between capturing and communing with the wilderness; between experiencing raw nature and wishing to domesticate it. To authentically experience nature truly you must live in it and be in harmony with it. So too, with your dreams.

Anxiety

It is hard to sustain anxiety without an internal dialog. Verbal dialog is notably absent in most dreams. In these dreams we do not reflect on the reality of the dream we're having. In dreamtime, we are hypnotized observers.

We normally think of dialog as something verbal, but there are other kinds. Visual dialogs occur in scenes without words, where situations are compared in contrast or pantomime. Kinesthetic dialogs occur where there is a play of the senses, as in tennis, sex, or in reflecting on the turning of the seasons. Dreams are rife with nonverbal dialogs. It seems we have exhausted verbal dialog in waking life. I suggest the first step in dream recollection is removing all of our dialog—verbal and nonverbal—and in that way dispelling the anxiety that could otherwise frighten us from the full experience.

A waking, nonverbal dialog is mindful or contemplative. We describe it as dreamy. Consider this as an approach to sleep and to lucidity in particular: to live a dreamier life. This leads to greater dream recollection, as you are in a state more consonant with dreams. Setting your intent to observe and participate, rather than record and analyze, helps you enter the flow of dreams. The purpose of the dream lies in what's happening and what you feel about what's happening, it's not embedded in an analysis of feelings and events separate from the experience.

Ego

Ego is an irregular porous boundary of the conscious self whose purpose is self-protection. It acts first as a presentation, second as a filter, and third—when there is time to reflect—as a judge. Most of our "free will" is directed toward how we present ourselves; it's debatable how much control we have over the course of events. Much of the ego's filtering is automatic; a minority of its decisions are considered.

It might be fair to say that dreams patrol the ego, repairing, rebuilding, and replacing behaviors and attitudes to maintain consistency. Dreams create the landscape of our emotion. But the dream process does not have direct control. Dreams can make you anxious, ambivalent, or inclined, but your ego still has the authority to act.

In a contest of inner wills, emotion wins over intellect, but one's inner mind is a medieval court of confederation, intrigue, and collusion. The ego governs action, but the subconscious governs perception and emotion. There is always some conflict, though one hopes it is creative. Destructive inner conflicts can manifest psychosis. Approach dreams with respect for the powers at work.

Think of ego as a membrane between your outer and inner self with keyed portals for through-passage. Biological membranes have myriad portals responding to unusual keys. Just as we thought we understood membranes—and we think we understand our egos—it turns out we understand neither.

As the biochemistry of cells interact, employ, and allow passage through membranes under different circumstances, so the ego, normally seen by us as the shell of our personality, has unexpected passageways between the outside world and our inner consciousness. There are backdoors, trapdoors, towers, moats, drawbridges, cellars, and dungeons.

Dreams explore the boundary of ego making ego uncomfortable. Dreams don't welcome the ego's interference, making lucidity potentially unhelpful, although it depends on which of your personalities is involved, or at what level of awareness you are lucid—an important point we'll explore later. There are ways for the ego to suggest dream content, and this is only natural. It can be done co-creatively in a way that is neither overbearing nor disruptive.

The spectrum of dream involvement begins with dream recollection—not to be dismissed as a minor affair—which we approach casually. Few know how to use dream recall for insight, but we will find much to make use of. Like first contact with an alien life-form, dream recollection is a Rosetta Stone for self-knowledge, far deeper than mindful self-contemplation. After all, we are talking about entering the land of visions.

Awareness

We're told we're conscious of 5% of our identity, and this is an overstatement. Like little boys bragging about their manhood, we are obsessed with thinking we're intelligent. I doubt we could even be aware of any more than a microscopic part of ourselves, but that may be irrelevant. What is relevant is the positive change we can foster in ourselves by becoming more aware of our ego's reality-filtering process.

The first step to enlarging awareness is to become comfortable in altered states. Forget the childish notion of linear lucidity, of there being a "more" and a "less." Focus instead on alternative forms of lucidity: what one is lucid of, and who is lucid, and how it is sustained. It is a common psychedelic experience to feel oneself lucid only to repeatedly have the bottom fall out and find yourself at another "level". Being lucid is a relative experience.

Focus on being present. Curtail the dialog. Dispense with the dichotomy. Aim to be an appreciated and well-behaved guest. Consider your dream as having the power to allow you to become lucid, rather than you having the power to awaken yourself in your dreams.

You will often be encouraged, in lucid dream tutorials, to get into the habit of testing your reality while awake and to let this habit of waking life bleed into your experience while dreaming, so testing becomes a normal thing you do. But real lucidity is not about waking up in dreams. Your subconscious will not accept this habit, if your ego's goal is self-entertainment. Reality testing will become habit only as a participatory process not an autocratic one. Aim to be an artist.

In our normal state, we distinguish ourselves from others and move to improve our position. In contrast, becoming more aware is a process of recognizing less difference, more similarity, and becoming more involved with what's around us. In the external world, we seek protection and advantage; in the internal world, risks and gains are different. In our internal world, advantage exists in relationships and understanding, not material things. Becoming mindful in the internal world involves courage and patience. We're looking for keys to the portals in the membrane of ego to open a passage to process and change.

Human consciousness is like dream recollection. It has been suggested that non-human consciousness is like our dream state, as it is without recollection or lucidity. That is to say, an animal's waking experience of reality is like our experience in dreams: everything is unquestionably real, everything is emotionally strong. Lucidity, and by association recollection, are highly organized processes within the prefrontal cortex—a process not in evidence when one is not lucid, in dreams or otherwise.

The consciousness of animals with a cerebral cortex but lacking a prefrontal cortex—which are non-primate mammals excluding birds, fish, reptiles, amphibians, and simpler classes for whom the discussion is more complex—is like our dream state. We can conjecture these non-primate mammals experience states of present awareness without ego, analysis, or a sense of past, and future. This is a state lacking both reflective and projective self, as well as lacking a sense of environmental control. Just to be clear: we're making a statement about the consciousnesses of primates and some non-primates—the ones with and the ones without a prefrontal cortex. I'm not saying anything about the consciousness of the other non-primates.

Human subjects with a propensity for lucid dreaming have a larger frontopolar cortex than humans subjects who don't. The frontopolar prefrontal cortex (Brodmann's area 10) is the frontmost area of the brain. It seems to contain the human brain's most advanced features, as it's twice as large, relative to the size of the whole brain, as similar areas found in other primates. Having the presence to explore one's dreams, either during or after the fact, is likely unique to primates. More than that, it appears to be something we are still in the process of evolving.

Clarity

To continue the parallel to waking life, self-reflection and stability are critical to lucid dreaming. Self-reflection is focused, measured awareness of the state of things. Stability is maintaining that state and letting distractions pass.

Having clarity doesn't necessarily entail lucidity, if lucidity is defined as taking control of the dream. That is not the target. We're aiming for insight and—as you know or may soon learn—excessive control is not insightful. Exerting less force often results in a more positive outcome. Yet, hands-off does not mean disconnected or uninvolved. The actions that yield the most positive results are felt, engaged, and intentional. To achieve this, one must develop and maintain clarity.

Developing clarity as a habit results in greater perspicuity and control in waking life, though that may not have been the original motivation. Once this habit is ingrained—so the theory goes—it will carry into your dreams. The result will not be greater control, but a more positive outcome within the existing limits of one's control.

Collaboration

In his book *Inner Work, Using Dreams and Active Imagination for Personal Growth*, Robert Johnson lists four steps to achieve revelation through dreams:

    1 - Associating dream elements with your waking experience.

    2 - Connecting dream elements with aspects of yourself.

    3 - Translating the dream's message into reflections on your life.

    4 - Taking action to set in memory the significance you feel.

If you do these things, or some variation of them, you will better remember your dreams, because you are facilitating your dreams. If you don't do these things, then your relationship with your dreams will remain incidental, and your dreams will lose interest in you.

In my efforts at lucidity I engage in these steps, and this seems to match the degree I am lucid in dreams. I believe this is generally true: lucidity—like breathing—is not a gift but an obligation, and the degree to which you participate is measured by the degree to which you play a role. And like breathing, the more you are willing to learn from the process, the more the process will reveal to you; and because of this, the more power and autonomy you will be accorded.

Guidance

An essential difference between inner and outer journeying is the inner journey's lack of the familiar. Every inner journey approaches the unfamiliar, as even the simplest dream illustrates.

If we are to be constructively aware and involved, we need direction over terrain that's unfamiliar and deeply personal, social, moral, historical, and ancestral. We need guidance. Call it what you will: intuition, higher wisdom, ancestors, power animals, or divine assistance.

You cannot get this from someone outside of yourself. No one can give it to you. No one can substitute for it. How do you get it? Through a simple and universal exercise: you ask for it. Will you get it? Not always. You need to know what you're asking for, and you need to be prepared. The following hypnotic session provides preparation and opportunity for this encounter.

> *"Dreaming is an unknown territory to many people. Historically, the dreamtime was as important to people as the waking hours. One of the reasons for the imbalance on the earth today is that so many people can't even remember, let alone work with, the material that comes to them in their dreams."*
>
> — Sun Bear, Wabun Wind, and Shawnodese, from *Dreaming with the Wheel.*

Hypnotic Session 2

Magic Hands audio file at:
https://www.mindstrengthbalance.com/becoming-lucid-audio/

Magic Hands

In the book *Dreaming with the Wheel*, Marlise Wabun Wind says:

"In a time so long ago, most people forget it ever existed, we all lived in the dreamtime. It did not matter whether we were awake or asleep... We could fly, we could talk to animals... We could go to the gods; we could part the waters. We could love wholly and completely... We lived within the web of life. With our eyes open, we could see and feel as much beauty as most people only feel today when they shut their eyes in sleep.

"Then time passed. With its passage, change occurred. We began to realize we were singular... We began to think. Our thoughts drove even more distance between us, and we drew apart in a way we never had before. We started to categorize, to measure... We lost our ability to speak to the animals... We could no longer feel the plants, or the minerals, or the elementals... Thoughts were different from the communications we had before... Our unity was never quite the same.

"One day a young one did something with her words that no one had ever done before... She used them to tell others about her dream. She said, 'Just close your eyes for a moment and remember.' And they did... They remembered, and they spoke. As they spoke, they wove that other reality into the reality that had become their everyday life. Come now and allow this circle to help you remember."

On the one hand, we knew what it was like to love wholly and completely, on the other hand, we think in words that keep us estranged. On the one hand, we could once recall deeper, older connections all around us. On the other hand, we began to awake to a future of our own construction that holds only what we have constructed. One hand sees inside and brings together, the other hand sees outside and sets things apart.

Now open your eyes and hold your hands out in front of you with the palms down… Think of the difference between your two hands, which we would otherwise think of as symmetric. There are small differences. The bend in your forearms, the angles of your wrists, the cant of hands, and the way you hold your fingers.

Can you feel the temperature in your hands? What is the extent of your sensations of temperature? Does one hand feel warmer and the other cooler… or is it the other way around? Move your palms. How does that affect the temperature of your hands?

Turn your hands over, palms up. Feel the temperature on the backs of your hands and on the palms of your hands. Which side feels warmer, the tops or the bottoms?

Consider the weight of each hand. Maybe one arm is stronger, so the hand on the stronger side feels lighter. Can you feel the weight of your two separate hands? Does one feel lighter than the other? Which hand is the lighter hand and which is the heavier?

Here's a psychological question, a question you might have to answer intuitively as much as by thinking... If you could imagine that one of your hands represented your child self and the other your grownup self... which one is more like the child, and which is more like the adult? What do you think about that?

Now, raise your hands so that the palms are facing you, at the width of your shoulders, palms at eye level. Look closely at the palms of your two hands, the shadows, shapes, textures, and topology of each palm. Look at them as if you were looking at them for the first time in your life. You feel a certain detachment from your hands, comparing them in an unusual fashion, looking at them in an unusual way.

And there is a certain strangeness in these questions and these examinations. A heaviness in their repetition that makes you feel relieved in letting your eyes relax. Allow your eyes to feel heavy and, with your hands still up in front of you, close your eyes, keeping a picture of your hands in your mind's eye, aware of their location in space.

Now I'd like you to consider the question of how you might remember a deeper connection with the world, and sense a deeper connection with the world... in your dreams. And consider which one of those hands is going to begin... really slowly now... to find its way onto your lap.

Consider actions you've taken, experiences you've had, dreams, memories, moods, or reflections you've had a deeper connection with when... your mind is open, and your thoughts extend to your whole awareness. And the intuition you have in knowing where to look and how to see things.

All of the connection you feel towards your inner self… the sense of allegiance and support… as if you were a team of different voices and visions, telepathically connected in thought, with respect and support… for the issues and insights of each part of yourself… reviewing and revealing to you, in sleep and dreams, the rhythm of things, and how they connect together.

As this hand continues to sink, what beliefs do you have about making a deeper connection? How has this affected you… through time, and how might it affect you in the future, and what you can do about deepening your connection. This one hand continues moving down to settle on your lap.

Let this hand relax comfortably in your lap, as you release whatever tension and sensation is in the arm that held it up. Fully relaxed now, comfortable and limp, like a cat purring, resting, and pleased.

Allow the idea to enter into your other hand, the image, and the energy of how you might learn from, and act from the insight and wisdom that forms in dreams, in the dreamtime, in the messages from dreams… coming as insight, reflection, and clarity in your waking life.

And this other hand, now, slowly… very slowly… starts to settle down toward your lap. Be open to hear, and to speak with, in day or night-time dreams, images of people, and energies… The dreamtime is an ever-present world… real or imagined, felt or thought, seen or sensed, from the present, the past, or from nowhere at all.

As this other hand settles down toward your lap, resting now comfortably in your lap, recall someone from your childhood, a family member, a friend, or even an animal that gave you strength, meaning, and resolve. Someone who gave you confidence and comfort, who allowed you to play in safety. Imagine a presence of comfort, grounded in deep feeling, a feeling that gives you guidance.

See yourself now in a wild field, outside a wild wood, under an evening sunset sky, clouds tinged like rainbows. The woods filled with animals, and you can see them hidden—using your mind's eye. Feel the wind beneath your arms, beneath your skirts, and be lighter. So light that the breeze lifts you, first off the ground, and then, lifted by a dust-devil, raised to the tree tops to see the woods from above.

Ask your mind, in your inner vision, who might be your guide and comfort for inner journeys. What image first comes to you? Who made you feel or in what place did you feel deeply yourself when you were very young? Maybe it's a time or place, and return there, and look around and see who is nearby. Be accepting, as in a dream, and let things come in any form, animate or inanimate, personal or impersonal, close, distant, real, or imagined.

Take this image of whomever, or whatever has come, and reflect on who was their guidance and who supported them. Now you must imagine, for sure, so let it form as an image assembled from feelings and fantasies: grandparents, ancestors, spirit animals, distant places, and peaceful moments.

See yourself now, here, in today's life, sensing what's around you, who's around you, and what's happening. Feel the wind beneath your arms and feel lighter to lift off the ground and to inject the free will to see beyond the walls of what you take for granted... the room, the building, city or town, toward the distant hills and quiet rivers... to have deeper understanding and a deeper connection with the world. And do this in waking life; a reasonable habit to acquire whatever sense of real you find or make for yourself.

Bringing yourself back slowly, but not altogether, leave parts of you in those cracks of deeper connection. Don't fail to remember the reality of what you imagine you can do. Remember the things you might think you cannot do that are only pictures of things you have not yet done but could, some way, some other way now, or as soon as you're ready to start. Solutions perhaps, but intuition by necessity. And what you dream you can, should, or might do is a form of insight with guidance. Things to dream up and to conjure or call when you next recognize that your dreams ask for your participation, for you to come in, and your guide to come with you.

When you're ready take a breath... inhale... exhale. Sense the stretch of your skin and the air around you. When you're ready, but not too quickly, regain your sense of direction, sense of balance, sense of time. Being ready to open your eyes. Counting to three: one... two... three. Loosely open your eyes... to be back... here... in this place.

Having Dreams

3 Finding Meaning

(In the dream's home territory) "Thinking moves in images, resemblances, correspondences. To go in this direction, we must sever the link with the dayworld, foregoing all ideas that originate there—translation, reclamation, compensation. We must go over the bridge and let it fall behind us, and if it will not fall, then let it burn."

— James Hillman, from *The Dream and the Underworld*.

Before talking about meaning, let's talk about kinds of meaning. Let's distinguish the path from the map; the meaning of a series of symbols versus the notion of meaning in general. This is the difference between getting to "a point" as opposed to discussing all possible points. This is a fundamental distinction that comes whenever there is a thing separate from the whole.

There are different schools of thought regarding dreams. They roughly break into those who subscribe to the idea that a dream has a message and those who advocate seeing the dream as a representation of one's whole state of affairs. If the first approach is right, then some of a dream's symbols are more essential and others less so. If the second approach is right, then not only are all symbols essential, but symbols might have different, supporting, contradictory, and simultaneous meanings. In the first case, there is a possible ideal path to get the meaning of a series of symbols. In the second case, there is not.

Because those who argue these points are not logicians, they fail to understand that these two perspectives are necessary and complementary parts of any whole that can be differentiated into parts. If dreams are an attempt to cognize the whole of our experience, then by mathematical laws both interpretations must be true. If there is a connected whole, then all paths will be necessary to understand the whole of it. Dreams are an attempt both to tell multiple possible stories and to frame some kind of "whole story."

The first aspect of dream interpretation is understanding the parts. The second is to understand the whole. I'll address them in this backwards order, because it makes manifest the questionable notion that we can, should, or need to interpret dreams at all. Interpreting our dreams has always been a natural inclination; we hardly have a choice in the activity of interpretation. You can't ignore dreams, you can only forget them.

> "... an implicit habit is to view dreams as text, the so-called unopened letters that must be properly read... each time we engage in the reading of a text, we do so from a given perspective, and we project into the text our presuppositions."
>
> — Fariba Bogzaran and Daniel Deslauriers, from *Integral Dreaming, A Holistic Approach to Dreams.*

Interpretation: Assembling the Parts

The interpretive approach is a linear and reasoned approach. You apply some initial perspective to extract meaning from a dream. Two things need to be defined before we follow this path: symbols and fractals.

Symbols

A symbol, according to Joseph Campbell in *Myths to Live By*, is,

> "... an image that hits where it counts. It is not addressed first to the brain to be interpreted and appreciated. On the contrary, if that is where it has to be read, the symbol is already dead. An 'affect image' talks directly to the feeling system and immediately elicits a response, after which the brain may come along with its interesting comments."

Symbols are composed of symbols. In my experience, in dreams I recall, I either see my symbol as something with a boundary, such as an image, or I feel what the symbol conveys as a whole. Consciously or not, I attend to the symbol's resonance in me, considering active, as well as secondary, circumstantial, or even incidental associations. By this process of taking-to-heart, I find my senses amplified, so as to be more aware of the implications of things.

Every trait portrayed in our dreams exists in us. Every character that appears in a dream reflects an aspect of us—though not necessarily attributes we are attracted to or accept about ourselves. Every character is an aspect of ourselves, and every attitude our characters express are attitudes that reside somewhere within us.

If a thief appears in a dream, says Robert Johnson in his classic *Inner Work*,

> "It doesn't literally mean you are a thief... it may be that you have been dishonest with yourself... The image of the thief may also mean that you have repressed some fine quality in yourself... and the only way it can get back into your life is to break in."

Every meaningful element is symbolic, and dreams are entirely composed of meaningful elements. The thief is meaningful, but so is the reason the thief is there. All details in the dream are important: what the character is doing, how it's dressed, its shape, movements, face, and hands. How the character acts in the environment, how the environment reacts to them. Unlike the real world, where many elements are incidental, there is nothing incidental in your dreams. In dreams, anything unimportant is left out.

As you recall a dream, you will probably be inventing some features in your waking recollection. That is, you will be filling in new elements that were left out in the dream. The dream is not an historical phenomenon—obviously it's inaccurate—it is also a creation of the present, at the time when you are remembering it. You're attempting to recreate the dream from memory, but as you are now reflective and trying to impose an understanding that was unnecessary when you were asleep, the experience of the dream won't be the same as when you were asleep.

It is worth noting that most elements of your current waking reality are also symbols. Not everything you perceive, but the elements that you apperceive. Apperception is the process of making sense of what you perceive. It's the process of recognizing what you're looking at.

You're only likely to remember what you recognize. The rest of what you perceive—people, objects, actions that you don't bother to make sense of—is quickly forgotten. Yet even these symbols, the ones you may not fully recognize, reflect aspects of yourself.

What you see of people and in people—the good, bad, attractive, repulsive, admirable and despicable—are aspects you have recognized in consideration of yourself. Every dream character reflects who you are but so do the characters in your waking life. Perception and inviting the world into our perception are creative acts. The closer you look at things, the more you're likely to see and the same holds true in dreams. We're trying to develop a habit of looking closely in dreams, and to do this, it's suggested, we look deeper into our waking life.

Fractals

Fractals are patterns that contain within themselves aspects of the whole of which they are a part. A fractal image, object, or symbol is a repeating motif, not in sequence like paper dolls but in scale like a cloud. Dream elements are fractals. Although the interpretive approach to dreams is reductive, the things to which we are reducing the dreams—namely their elements—are whole elements in and of themselves. As such, the dream elements that we'll "extract" from the dream have resonances and associations inside them.

Dream elements are symbols; these symbols are fractals. The symbols are themselves composed of symbols. For example, a dream person is composed of symbolic attributes, just as a real person is: they may be attractive, young, and dynamic, or they may be the opposite. A building might be imposing, inviting, and full of activity, or it may be the opposite.

To say that like fractals, symbols are composed of symbols may sound confusing, but it is made simpler by recognizing that fractals display repetitive symmetry: the parts within them reflect the parts outside of them. The pattern is repeating, as the theme of the symbol is usually repeated in the themes of its elements. You might say the symbolic elements amplify each other to give the dream its "larger than life" character. This pattern is demonstrated in this brief description of one of my dreams:

I am climbing down a narrow, mountain path, leading from a pasture-like parking area, down into a lower gorge in which is located an airfield. The sky is thickly overcast the air is cold. It feels

Finding Meaning

like there is snow in the air. There is a small plane ready to take off on this airfield. I am carrying a large haphazard load down the path toward this airplane. I am in the airplane. I am the pilot. My gear is stowed. I am taking off, pressing hard on the right rudder, as the torque of the propeller accelerates me down the runway.

The symbols here include the pasture, the path, the load, the gorge, the weather, the airfield, the airplane, controlling the airplane, and the sky. These symbols hold particular meaning to me.

Moving alone and by foot from the parking area to cross a precipice reflects the same meaning as accelerating down a runway to become airborne. My transition from the pasture to the gorge reflects my transition from walking to flying. Carrying a precarious load down a steep trail has the same feeling as attempting to take off into a stormy overcast. The car-trail-plane triad reflects the driving-walking-flying triad. This recapitulation of messages makes the dream more impressive, focused, and emotional. Unlike waking life, the dream has no extraneous symbols.

The experience of this dream was that of a series of symbolic cameos or short film clips. The content of each visual was small. As you should be aware, the size of the area that you see with your eyes is also small. It's a circle in your field of view that subtends approximately a 1-degree arc, which is the size of your thumb held at arm's length.

Outside of this small circle lies your fuzzy peripheral vision. We proceed through our waking life hardly being aware of how little we see, and it's the same in a dream, except in a dream the details that we overlook are not even there. Becoming lucid in a dream means, among other things, that you may have a lot of filling in to do, filling in that was previously unnecessary.

What you do see in dreams are the symbols. The symbols'

meanings are recapitulated by the order in which they appear. This is another example of the fractal property of symbols within symbols. Important, too, are the sights and sounds captured in the dream: the agoraphobic feeling of teetering over a precipice; the vertiginous feeling of accelerating into a turbulent sky. Feelings are symbols too.

Within each of these symbols—such as I might remember them or weave them from memory after the fact—are further details. I don't know whether I was unaware of these details when I experienced the dream, and I am noticing them now or whether these details never existed in the dream, and I am creating them now, as I put myself back into the experience. In either case, these details clarify the dream and amplify its effect on me.

Think of entering a cathedral in waking life. Everything you experience attempts to convey the majesty of God, the insignificance of man, and the power of the church: the towers, the pillars, the arches, the statuary, the transition of spaces, the light, sound, textures, textiles, furniture, even the pillows and holy books. Each symbol, down to the smallest detail, recapitulates the message. You would not expect, for example, the holy books to have product endorsements or bookmarks with pictures from Angry Birds or Jurassic Park!

It is like this with a dream: each symbol within the dream reflects the whole not just part of it. This is similar to a hologram, as each piece of the hologram contains a rough picture of the whole. Assembling the pieces of a hologram does not create a bigger picture, it creates a more detailed picture.

> *"If you focus your attention, in as intense and coherent a manner as possible, on the dream, the image of the dreamer will be revealed in multidimensional detail. This is true even if, as with the broken holographic plate, you have only been able to remember a fragment of*

the dream... When you take a fragment of a dream and focus intensely on it, you produce an image of the dreamer that is multidimensional and will include an awareness of the forces that helped to create the dream."
— Shawnodese, from *Dreaming with the Wheel.*

This partly explains why dreams lack a past and future. Past and future are encapsulated in the dream itself. The dream is not a segment existing in time but a commentary on all that occurs in time's passing.

"If you apply the dream on the external level, it usually turns out to be superficial... If you take your dreams as a reflection of the unconscious dynamics within, you are most likely to get to the heart of the matter... It is at the inner level that your dream is usually aimed."
— Robert Johnson, from *Inner Work, Using Dreams and Active Imagination for Personal Growth.*

Active Imagination

Jung's technique of active imagination asks the dreamer to return, in waking, to the dream space and there to participate in imagery, emotions, and experiences. The dream is easy to re-enter, because you can restart it from any point; starting at any part restarts the whole thing.

Upon waking but before entirely waking, project yourself back, freezing progression, as if ceasing to reknit the whole. Focus on the stitches, the symbols. Relax, hold each image, and from within each, sense the theme of the whole complex situation in which you find yourself embedded. And this is important: find yourself embedded not "had found yourself embedded." You are reentering the present not recalling the past. This is the realm where lucidity can be applied, a restored lucidity, from which the whole dream calliope begins to turn again.

Symbolic amplification takes one back in trance to the root feeling underlying the dream's texture. Maintain presence, suspend engagement and, with intent, turn the corner, move down the path, and open whatever door you find. As you do, imagine the meaning behind each symbol while, at the same time, asking for greater insight into the meaning of each.

Upon waking, the process of writing your recollection will braid extensions into the dream. After interrupting the dream, with the intention to return to sleep, you'll enter a kind of lucidity, one in which you will have some control. You might then lose control as the dream restarts or maintain it to some extent.

Lucidity is a matter of degree. As long as there is some measure of dreaming, you are not in full control. To be in full control is to be fully awake which reduces the dialog with your subconscious mind to the monologue with yourself. Dreaming is a relationship not a monopoly. Apply active imagination at any time, as no dream is too old that it will not respond when recalled and analyzed using meanings and associations.

Holism

Your subconscious mind is a collection of needs you must support for you to prosper. Your conscious mind is a collection of strategies you employ to meet these needs. When your conscious mind is unable to meet the needs of your subconscious mind, you become neurotic. When your conscious mind attacks the needs of your subconscious mind, you become psychotic. Dreams provide you with the opportunity to take a more active role in this reconciliation.

Finding Meaning

I see two parts to any holistic interpretation: not being attached to the parts and not being attached to a plot line. Being non-attached means being open minded and willing to bend definitions, interpretations, expectations, and conclusions. There needs to be a certain degree of humor here. A freedom to throw away everything you think and be left with something simpler.

Eschewing a plot line is being open to transformation, chaos, or opportunity. In linear plots, which are plots that progress sequentially in time, transformation enters as something that's developing: a threat, conflict, or opportunity. The same result can be obtained following a simple and certain path that spontaneously—and nonlinearly—diverges, elevates, or explodes to a different level.

In mystery novels and in logic miracles are considered cheating, but leaps of faith are commonplace in dreams. One might argue that such ruptures of reason make the most sense where the storyline was a fantasy to begin with. Sometimes, a reality-check can have a miraculous effect. I believe this is a salient description of our personal realities.

> *"In the non-interpretive approach, the dream remains a living creation constantly changing and evolving into new horizons... Dream understanding becomes a process that is changeable when viewed from different perspectives... Refrain from directing how the dream unfolds."*
>
> — Fariba Bogzaran, Daniel Deslauriers, from *Integral Dreaming, A Holistic Approach to Dreams*.

The interpretive and the holistic perspectives are complementary in the understanding of dreams. Each provides a different language that can be used to describe the same dream content. The interpretive perspective attempts to find meaning by resolving causes and effects.

The holistic perspective considers the whole network of influences to discern overall patterns. This is fundamental to the complementarity between the whole and its parts.

If your interpretations are correct, then the conclusions of one should support the other. At the same time, the degree to which your impressions diverge is a measure of how independently you are pursuing the two perspectives. This is to be welcomed for the insight it provides.

Superposition

There is another essential layer of multiplicity. A fundamental insight from quantum mechanics insists that all descriptions of nature must be assembled by overlaying exclusive alternatives. This is called superposition, as it super imposes distinct and separate alternatives. These are possibilities that are compatible with what we know for certain but are incompatible with each other.

A simple example is getting from here to there. There are many paths, and they are different. You cannot take them all as you must choose one. A superposition of outcomes is what you obtain when you choose them all. This isn't possible in waking life as we navigate in the present, but it is a pretty good description of how we consider our options for the future: we weigh them all.

The paradigmatic example from physics is that of a single particle that can travel two separate paths from a known origin to a known destination. In the classical case, one path must be chosen; in the quantum case, both paths are traversed simultaneously, at least that is how we describe it after the fact.

In most cases there are a multitude of possibilities—many unlikely—and only one set of similar paths contribute to what we observe. In some cases—such as the transistor—dissimilar and incommensurate paths contribute to what we observe. The transistor is a quantum mechanical object and its inclusion in our everyday life has changed the world.

Competing alternatives exist within a given perspective such as different possible paths or different possible wholes. These alternatives appear to be exclusive, but they are not. Reality, as we know it in the physical world, is the result of combining all possible exclusive alternatives giving more weight to the more probable and less weight to the less probable. The fact that we have choices does make a difference, even if we must choose only one.

If it were not for superposition, the progression of things would sink into their most stable states and stay there forever. Things would never transition out of stasis of their own accord. They would never decay, and we would not have chemical reactions as we know it. We would be unable to claim free will, because everything would appear to be determined.

Recognize that alternative interpretations can be simultaneously true, even if they contradict each other. In *Inner Work*, Robert Johnson uses the word "energy" and says:

"Your dream is composed of energy systems... if (your) interpretation arouses energy and strong feelings in you... if you suddenly think of other areas in your life where this interpretation makes sense... (then) there is a tremendous energy behind this interpretation."

Quantum mechanics—which is not limited to microscopic physics—tells us to reject the single-cause approach to nature. Not only is a single cause fundamentally unknowable, but no single cause is sufficient to explain what we see. Single causes only seem to exist in those cases where one cause is overwhelmingly likely.

We like situations with single causes, situations where causality follows a single path. We seem to have one-track minds; we like to construct obedient situations. The ego is, after all, our organ of control. We like to see situations as having certain results as these situations are most amenable to linear thinking.

The reductionist assertion that one cause will always explain any experience works poorly in describing the behavior of collections of people. It works poorly in describing individual people who behave as a collection of attitudes. Reductionist thinking has little use in the realm of dreams. Here you must understand that many things are being presented at once, as in the following dream.

I am moving West, and I must decide where to go. I am living with my ex-wife, but we are not married. We are looking for a warmer place. We are exploring one location on a snow-covered hillside, but it will thaw in the summer. After much discussion and exploration, I accept it and think she does too, but she does not.

Moving far north to the Arctic becomes another alternative for us. This seems ridiculous to me, but now it seems attractive to her, so we agree on this location. We will move separately. We are vacating our house. It is already a rather sterile and empty house..

The new owners have moved in. I am trying to collect my last things. I am trying to determine whether my ex-wife has already left. I hear the phone ring and an answering machine pick up. It is a call on her line. I hear the recorded message playing from within the bathroom. The bathroom is stark, sterile, and dark. I am looking through the bathroom cupboards, but they are empty. I cannot find the answering machine.

This shortened version of the dream illustrates the multiplicity common in dreams. Interpreting this dream is not an exercise in finding the one path that puts its varying elements in order but rather a collecting of thought fragments in order to assemble a "reality

Finding Meaning

collage" of my feelings, decisions, thoughts, and state in life. Dreams are chaotic systems; adding more detail does not make them simpler it makes them larger.

In this dream, there are feelings of remorse and uncertainty, disappointment and need, assertion and helplessness. There are symbols of collaboration and indifference, attraction and rejection, mixed with feelings of conclusion and chaos, loneliness, hope, and alienation. The one thing that could be said is that this is a dream concerned with transition and depression. To reduce this dream to a linear narrative echoes Woody Allen's joke that, after mastering the art of speed reading, all he can recall is that Tolstoy's War and Peace was a book about Russia.

The dream contains linear elements. I recall searching through the empty cupboards of the dreary, white-tiled bathroom looking for an old answering machine that was not there. The dream had a reasonable plot line, but this line was not followed reasonably.

This dream's structure was more than the sum of its parts. It was clearly both a reflection on the past and an examination of the future collecting emotions from both directions. The truth of the dream overlays all these ideas. Each vignette tracing different thoughts and feelings assembled into a whole—the result is the emotions I am left with.

There is no guarantee you can "understand" your dreams. James Hillman, a leader in dream psychotherapy, admonishes us to approach dreams on their own terms. Taming dreams for the benefit of conscious understanding reduces them to a taxidermist's diorama. To Hillman, the prejudice of the waking mind is a hindrance to being with the dream. Like reducing a culture to a study of its language rather than entering the culture to speak with it, to understand the dream we must live it. We must see with the dream's eyes. If this results in the dream's lack of making conscious sense, then this is part of the message.

Understanding

What are usually referred to as methods of dream interpretation are methods of selective remembering. Their application embodies the danger of interpreting any text: you only understand what lies within the scope of what you see.

If to "understand" is to make rational sense, then I agree with Hillman: you cannot understand any dream. The subconscious is not just hidden, it is incomprehensible in linear form. However, I believe we can appreciate the subconscious enough to collaborate with it. That's what consciousness is for.

Three ideas crucial to this collaboration are the complementarity of the interpretive and holistic approaches, the superposition of multiple messages, and the fractal nature of dream symbols. The result of applying these ideas simultaneously is to greatly expand our appreciation of dreams.

Embedded in your dream is a reflection of yourself, your attitudes about yourself, your relation to the world, your sense of place in the world, your sense of purpose, and your attitude toward life. These things are embodied in your consciousness all of the time, but in dreams the practical exigencies of the moment are absent, and everything is an internal reflection. The dream is, essentially, all of you magnified. Your different consciousnesses reflects on themselves, in the context of recent episodes, and your memory of past experience.

The next time you have a vivid dream, I challenge you to write it down in complete and uncensored detail: to examine and report on every foreground, background, emotion, reference, insight, and association. I suspect this will be a never-ending process and at some point, you will have to declare your time and energy exhausted and your effort incomplete.

After spending several hours exploring his imagination in a waking trance, Nick, a client of mine, reported:

> "I encountered an unexpected unfolding of deep symbols and images. Scenes that I wouldn't have believed I could imagine but that were somehow right and familiar organically grew out of each other. Most of the images were not what you would call pleasant or radiant, but they gave me the reassuring feeling that there was much more to me than I had been aware... What was buried came to light... I went out and all creative blocks were broken for three days."

I expect that if you were to pursue your dream "to the ends of the earth," as it were, you would encounter strange, uncomfortable, inspiring, and unexpected images.

> "The whole of life is a succession of dreams. My ambition is to be a conscious dreamer, that is all."
>
> — Swami Vivekananda

Hypnotic Session 3

Tapestry audio file at:
https://www.mindstrengthbalance.com/becoming-lucid-audio/

Tapestry

The purpose of this exercise is to amplify the detail in the images you imagine. To fill in, expand, and extend details where you might otherwise be satisfied with less. To build bigger and more intentional daydreams so that you develop a habit of asking for, and receiving, more detail in night-time dreams. And to explore the idea that you might be aware of your own creative process, watching yourself like an audience, without disturbing the master at work.

Find a relaxed position; arms and legs uncrossed and well supported. Let your eyes relax and close, as this exercise begins.

Let me politely ask you to stop your chattering mind by listening to your body. And if you do focus on some part of your body to quiet your mind, you will find there are other parts of your mind, like the defiant members of a reluctant classroom, that continue to whisper among themselves. Let me politely ask those members of your mind for their attention, too, and let me help them to do that by giving them some tasks to perform.

First, I want you to focus on your attention, not with it, but on it. I want you to see how you hear my words and feel how they break on your awareness in waves. These are not the waves of sound, though waves of sound do break on you. These are waves of your awareness.

Finding Meaning

Become aware that your hearing of my voice comes in separated rapid-fire units of attention. These units arrive a bit slower than the frames of movie which are too fast to distinguish. You can discern these units, if you step back and notice the texture of your awareness. It's dappled like peanut butter spread over a rough cracker; your awareness is a texture of relative and rapid-fire engagements.

Feel this now. It's as fast as the vibration you feel when you're being shocked by a kitchen appliance. It's that fast, and it would be that disruptive too, if you hadn't learned to recognize it as awareness. Let those truant voices in the back of your mind be given the task of paying close attention to the sawtooth details of their own attention.

Second, let those sitting in your mind's front row—and maybe there is one of you, but probably there are several inside your head—follow the base note rhythm that is your breathing. That slow and paced rise and fall... inhale... and exhale...

Really attend to the shape of this waveform as it swells, crests, flattens, and relaxes. It then deflates in a straight line; first relieving your biggest muscles, and then the smaller muscles, until your chest has settled, and whatever air remains leaks out of you of its own accord.

But keep the back row of your mind focused on your ragged attention, ragged even in attending to yourself. After all, this ragged attention is in your brain and of your consciousness.

And third, let the rest of your classroom of mind—all the other insistent voices, indifferent tissues, insouciant attitudes— pay attention to the details of your pulse. Follow them across your body like the waves you stir up across the surface of your bathtub.

Listen to your pulse within your body. And if you can't hear it, then imagine it, and count it out to yourself picturing a metronome inside you. And what do you think governs that metronome in your imagination? It's your heart, the same one you might think you cannot hear.

The simplest juggling involves three balls and full relaxation involves engaging three distractions: your breath… your pulse… and your attention. Inhale, beat-beat-beat, pause… Exhale, beat-beat-beat, pause…

Hold these now in your focus, layered on each other, and keep them in the air. And as you have them airborne and cycling, relax your mind into full witness in your descent of this stairway:

Imagine ten stairs leading down into a forest, and you're at the top, and you're looking down, and paint the top stairs in your imagination, and see them first as clear and carefully carpentered, and then, halfway, becoming rough-hewn, less regular, and down at the bottom—but you haven't gotten there yet—they are just stones dug into the hillside.

10, 9, going down the clear and straight-edged stairs flat treaded with even risers. More relaxed with each step down, 7, 6. Now, down to the rough-hewn slightly irregular stairs and you must be more careful of your steps and to judge the distance and the height. 5, 4, and now they're irregular, no longer flat, and you must hold some tension in your ankles being aware of the balance of your body. 3, 2, almost down, as they are just stones now, and the stairs are but jutting rocks. And one, you're down,

Finding Meaning

and now relax, as the path is smooth at least, still leading down, but effortlessly.

Look around you, and as you do so, let images drop into your mind without effort. Simply say a word or two to yourself and see what comes: "woodland trees" or "forest trail" or "blue sky." Project yourself onto some park trail or forest path that you remember, and look around. Where you look ideas and images appear, and if they don't that is good, too. Let the blank spots be. Some things form more slowly. Be patient.

See yourself moving through the woods, around a corner, then around another. Imagine the sounds, and you can sense their direction but usually not their origin. Trees creak, leaves rustle, birds call.

You arrive at a clearing maybe 50 feet across. Circular in shape with large trees evenly spaced around the perimeter. The space cleared and flat, covered with low grasses and small shrubs. The crowns of the trees almost touching to create a kind of roof, a very tall, cathedral-like space.

And as you scan the trees you notice that some of the tree trunks seem to have doors embedded in them. Closely fitted, narrow, single doors. Some crested, maybe square, some hidden by their natural color, others might be bright. And as you walk around and inspect each trunk more closely, you see that every tree has a door of some kind. And there are knobs or handles evident on most and steps up to the doors, maybe a stone step, raised earth, or a root.

And you can pick one door, one that seems to attract your attention, maybe it's the color or the shape, or the patterns around it, or the tree itself, tall and slender, or old and gnarled. Approach this tree with its door, and stop in front of it just to marvel at what you've been able to create—the detail you've recalled just from your memory and imagination. Look twice at the tree in front of you, and see it both in the detail of its bark and the overall sense of the whole. Patterns in the leaves overhead and details in the earth around its trunk.

Step up to the door. Consider what you feel about the comfortable curious world that lies beyond it. Reach out and touch the door knob, handle, or latch, and appreciate this connection, for a moment, between the image of your hand, yourself, the door, and the tree. Then open the door to reveal a clean, clear, shaded interior. Step through the door. You are inside the tree. Close the door behind you and in your mind's ear say "closed."

You're in a warm small but very tall room. You have the comfortable feeling of being tucked in beneath a warm quilt, safely held with fresh moving air and a tunnel in front of you that leads out toward what you can see of bright sun and blue sky.

Move down this tunnel, too dark to see much to either side, as the bright blue sky at its opening blinds you. And find yourself emerging through a hole in the earth, onto a grassy hillside, high above a wide valley. And look around you and ask for details to appear. To the left... to the right... what do you see? Tattered clouds, a breeze that brushes your face or tousles your hair. A tall sky reaches back, blindingly blue, overhead, and a mist collects in the distance to blur what appears on the other side and down the valley.

And what do you see on the other side? And what is there down the valley to the left, and then turn to the right, and the scene paints itself. What appears to you? Examine the details. Ask questions, explore your feelings. What does this bring to mind?

What are you thinking about as you're creating it? Is it entirely your imagination, or is it a kind of memory projection colored by hopes and wishes? If the images are commanded, how about the feelings? Are they real or imagined?

See yourself walking down the hillside, down a path; work through the grass, a runnel of earth pressed by some huge, rolling, stone ball. Curved up on either side and evenly descending across the hillside like a marble raceway.

And come to a ravine, one of those deep creases in the hillside, cut by millennia of running water from the rain, off the hillcrest, somewhere high above you in the sunlit sky. And your path takes a sharp turn inward, and downward, into the earth, creased, folded, and twisted down into the brush and rocks like broken bones into an older place cut through layers of sediment.

Descend into this ravine and as your path descends, it gets steeper to make jags and turns and jumps around jutting rocks, twisted corners, and dropping slabs. And down and down… and take a breath and pause… before the relief of sliding into the cup of the next turn… and the wall that rises behind you folds in with the wall that rises before you… and down further as you pass around dark inside corners and balance around narrow outside corners.

Gaps between the rocks grow larger making small grottos—shallow but dim. Rarely lit in the sliver of sky that is all the ravine affords. But your sun is overhead, and the twisting trail shimmers in the sun's spotlight, and light bounces all around like reflections from a disco ball, and you pass more shallow overhangs with rock benches and openings like vestibules and passageways.

Come to one that's unusually flat-floored like a deep resting area, chisel cut, secure, with comfortable rocks for benches and virtually no view of the sky, just light reflected, at just this time of day, feeling like a cozy cabin living room. And stop, and sit, and explore it.

It's another tunnel, another cave entrance, illuminated by the light. And what color is the floor, and what color are the walls, and what appears to decorate it? Are there vines, bushes, roots? Are there leaves, buds, or flowers? What is the smell? Is it dusty or moist, dank or fresh? Use your imagination. Ask these questions. Listen to the answers however they come as sights or sounds, or better yet, as feelings and intuitions. Take nothing for granted, don't be satisfied. Explore. Ask questions.

Take a breath. Relax. Inhale… exhale…

As you enter into this tunnel, take a turn, climb a few steps, and find yourself transported immediately… into the desert. A broad expanse of flat landscape opened to either side from the shallow swale out of whose steps you've climbed. A world of sand and scrub and dusty air moving like a smooth ocean with nothing to disturb its even airy flow. Look around. Look at your feet.

Look into the distance. What do you see on the horizon? Is it a flat and purple tableau of deep sky and wisps of cloud? Is there a plateau? Maybe a dark line at the buttes edge along the desert

Finding Meaning

floor. Maybe there are mesas, or the Grand Canyon, dropping out of site into wild and turning valleys. Examine what you cannot see using all your remote senses. Explore the subtle feelings of all the things that could be, given what you know, and what you don't.

Walking forward in this simple and foreign landscape with spindly thick leaved plants clinging weakly by one deep root. A layer of sand blowing across your feet—smoothing holes and filling in the ant hills. Creating rippled waves of dust like waves under the beach surf. And every now and then there is a swale, gully, old arroyo that carries water on that one day of the year it rains. You slip down to the hard pack and slog up the sliding sand on the other side.

Walk easily, hardly lifting your feet, more like swaying and floating. And relax and go deeper. Explore your own body for tensions that may have been caught or grown or built from ideas and images, and let those tensions go. Inhale… exhale…

Crest a small sand dune and on the other side, find a temple entrance. A portico buried to its roof, with carved pillars, long since sandblasted of any texture but smooth. Stop to examine the image you create of something like a bunker but with columns. Beside the entrance are worn rocks shaped like statuary. A square-edged cavern, pick a door, and enter, leaving the boundless desert sky behind. Feel yourself sliding forward into an ever darker, ever sharper echoed, squared sided chamber, a long anteroom, and wide hallway with its protected entrance, with hints of painted colors on its interior walls, fading behind you.

Hear the sea, and drop yourself forward into a liquid darkness with a faint light your eyes have yet to be accustomed to. Now you're in a water world, and what seemed like floating is floating, and there is nothing strange about it. You're just here, looking forward, watching dim shadows, and blinking your eyes to adapt to its dimness.

What was air is now water, and what was dry in your throat is now liquid, distilled, and reviving. You move horizontally, face forward, like a fish. And you move in undulations with your whole body, with your fishtail and fin-like arms. It's a kind of flying without gravity. Aerodynamic without air.

Explore the novelty. Explore the details. As things get stranger, what can you imagine? Can you fill in as many details? What is there to see and hear where you cannot? Remember swimming under the water. Maybe you opened your eyes or wore a mask, and what could you see or imagine you saw?

The water is thick; light doesn't travel far. Darkness prevails not too far away in any direction. Light comes from above, dappled and broken. The surface like a shifting mirror of wave convexities, rippling, tippling, and bouncing. Reflecting and refracting, giving speckled shafts and spots of light. Showing and hiding, rocks and plants, fish and faces.

This is a world of sound, one for which we have little memory, but it is a world as rich and detailed as our own. Make it as rich and detailed as the topside world we live in. Take the brush of your imagination, and paint in what could be there. There is a distance, a topography, hills and valleys even if you cannot see them.

You've listened under water beneath the ocean waves. You

remember how loud it is, as clicks and snaps like bat radar surround you. The fish are listening to the sights around them, and knowing with ear-sight who is coming and who is going away. What if you saw with your ears, what would you see? Imagine you could do this too, that you had an image of shapes from far away, just from the sound they reflect.

And you are moving forward, languid and effortless, moving with your body. You are relaxed, and you breathe the water. Inhale... exhale...

You are coming to the shoreline, and mostly there is shale and shingle rising into shallows. There are also streams that come to your sea, and these exhale fresh water courses into this water world like great conduits of air ventilating the sea. Water burrows extending arm-like into the land, to part the beach, to make a path you want to follow. Perhaps like a salmon you remember and recognize one to be familiar.

Swim up in these outlets, moving out of the ocean into an inlet. Follow its narrowing course as it becomes a shallow stream, river, or brook coursing around rocks and boulders, and you navigate easily as the water holds you to the center stream.

Now the world is thin, flat, and turbulent. You're buffeted, and pushed, and bounced. Can you examine your world while you're creating it? Can you reflect and perceive when the perceptions are themselves reflections? If this was a dream, could you be lucid in it? What would you do if you could? You might say, "Let the river become a lake," and it would become a lake. And now you are in a lake swimming through cold and shallow waters toward a tideless beach. And you are belly on the sand.

Flip your way forward, head above water, big goggle eyes taking in 360 degrees.

And now you say, "Become a person again." And little feet sprout from where there were fins and like a tadpole on spindly legs and thick tail, you prop yourself up, growing up, to crouching as your tail shrinks. And you're a frog crouched, eyes blinking, flop bellied, as your knees grow larger, sitting now on your haunches. Take a deep breath through your nose. Inhale… exhale…

Lean forward and your legs take your weight and with a glance down, you can stand, now on two feet, your arms hanging, air caressing your ankles and wrists. You were naked and barefoot in your rapid aquatic fish evolution, and clothes appear, walking up the beach to an unpaved, lakeside road.

The world is familiar again, and you stop at the road and imagine all the drab and familiar things roads bring: cars, people, twigs, gravel, litter, the distant sounds of motors. Walk down the road. There's nothing to see, just the lake, the curb, the woods, and a crossroad. A corner like any other. You make a right turn, gravel rustling beneath your shoes, and there are buildings in the distance. And you keep walking. An empty summer day, and the world keeps turning, time measured only by the tumble of leaves and the sun.

You've come to a small town, with just a few small shops, a park, a church. There is a coffee shop and you go in it and transition to a different world of light and sound.

It's full of people. They are familiar. You take a table. Look around. What's on the walls, what's out the window? Look at the

Finding Meaning

people. Move from face to face. Old, young, couples, workmen, kids.

See a child. Describe the child you see. How old are they? How are they dressed? What would you guess about them? How do you know them? Can you imagine the answers as fast as I can invent the questions? Maybe even faster, seeing things I can't describe.

See a young woman sitting at the counter. Describe her. Is she familiar? What is her name? What does she do? What does she think? How does she feel? You're making this up. How do you feel? Are you making that up?

See a young man. What does he look like? Describe the young man. What is his age? Does he see you? Does he know you? Does he have a story? You rise, leave some change, and head for the coffee shop's back door. You exit through the back door.

Behind the coffee shop there is a large garden full of blooming trees and shrubs. In the center, there is a stone church. You are in the garden, walking past the blooming flowers, the wavering grasses, the bud-laden fruit trees. You approach the church. It's a dark grey stone church, solidly built, not that big but big enough.

Enter the stone church. Its stone lintel passing overhead. Through the entryway, you enter the nave with its rows of aisles. Ahead is the altar. Describe the place. How does it make you feel? In the sanctuary, you find a comfortable armchair. Move to it, and sit in it relaxed and supported.

Think about the parts of this journey—ocean, river, desert,

forest—the tone in each. Which were more detailed? Which were less? Which were more curious or more exciting, more relaxing?

Was there a pervasive feeling? Could you always feel yourself? Can you think about what your imagining, and still have the freedom to imagine? Does thinking throw you off-track? Is there a way that you can think that would not disturb your imagination? Do you have one mind that talks, and one mind that paints, and one mind that is not there at all?

Now come back. I'll count to 10, and as I count up. Leave the images behind you evaporating like a long past vacation. 1… 2… 3… Keep only a few images, souvenirs, mementos. 4… 5… 6…. Feeling clear. Feeling balanced, with health and energy. 7… 8… 9… Open your eyes when you're ready, 10. Returning to the present.

Finding Meaning

4 Being Lucid

"(When you realize you are) programming everything that is happening inside your head... you can go to the limits of your conceptions."
— John C. Lilly (1915-2001)

"If you can change your mind, you can change your life."
— William James (1842 - 1910)

Sleep States and Frames of Mind

Consider three states of mind: present, reflective, and personally detached. We move between these in our normal waking state, and these states also occur in our experience of dreams. We switch between them quickly in normal waking state. We mostly experience dreams in the state of presence, occasionally admitting a limited form of reflection, and only rarely becoming detached. We consider these three states here because it helps us communicate and negotiate lucidity. I do not claim these divisions are unassailable or absolute.

The process of moving out of one state and into the next is the process of becoming lucid. Lucidity is an action or transformation.

We experience each of these states in waking or sleeping consciousness. Becoming lucid is a process of "leveling up" to the next more aware state. As each state is different, so the lucidities that carry one out of each state differ. There are, therefore, three different kinds of lucidity: moving from present to reflective, from reflective to detached, and moving from detached to wherever that takes you. We'll consider that fourth state in the last chapter. Full lucidity is the facility to voluntarily move between each.

We might say we have three different subconscious minds depending on which part of our brain's subconscious we are communicating with. Or, we might say that our one subconscious has three different conversations, depending on which conscious state it is engaged with. Our different states of mind ask different questions and process answers differently; much as we speak differently to people of different ages, animals of different species, or people on other levels of consciousness.

These states have different mental focus and self-awareness. Focus and self-awareness are key features, keys to critical thinking, and they largely lie outside of our language and social dialog. They are key because we can enhance them if we recognize the inadequacy of our language to describe them, and then we might repair this inadequacy. By describing to ourselves what is taking place in our thoughts, we gain lucidity. This carries over into dreaming.

Becoming Lucid

> *"In your imagination you begin to talk to your images, and interact with them. They answer back. You are startled to find out that they express radically different viewpoints from your conscious mind. They tell you things you never consciously knew, and express thoughts that you never consciously thought."*
> — Robert Johnson, from *Inner Work*.

If you want to develop dream lucidity, work to improve the fluency of conversations you have with yourself. It has been noted that your recollection of dreams may decrease if you actively explore your subconscious while awake, but you can increase dream recollection by waking up during dreams, and by collecting dream memories through journaling.

It is said that we mostly dream in REM sleep, but people woken from any stage of sleep may remember dreams. I suspect we dream much of the time. We certainly do when we're awake. We're familiar with the hypnagogic images of Stage 1 sleep where intrusive scenes are sometimes short cameo appearances. These dreams are fleeting, fragmented, and center on feelings, emotions, and drives. They can be tamed and invited to develop into full dreams.

Stage 1

Stage 1 sleep is the hypnagogic state. It's the realm of hypnosis, a realm amenable to awareness and lucidity. You can speak aloud in this level of hypnosis. Daytime anxieties and expectations, manifesting as tension in Stage 1, keep us awake until they remit. We can take control of our subconscious using active imagination, as we enter Stage 1.

"Staying alert and watching hypnagogia build and morph is an

excellent practice for learning the art of entering a lucid dream from the waking state, and it also helps you stay lucid in a dream when the scene starts to flicker and dissolve... Even just altering the direction of your gaze while hypnagogia-watching can be enough to send all the images scattering like frightened fish.

"If the image is stable enough to withstand your direct, conscious gaze, it will likely grow stronger and even stranger, and you'll be able to guide its development with your thoughts and expectations. If you stay calm and focused, the imagery will take the leap into three-dimensionality, and you'll be awake inside your dream."
— Clare Johnson, from *Llewellyn's Complete Book of Lucid Dreaming.*

Stage 2

We spend the most of our sleeping time in non-REM Stage 2 sleep. I observe dreams in Stage 2 sleep to be of the present sort. That is, they seem to happen in the first-person and are relatively linear in their progress. These dreams occur as we transfer events into long-term memory and, I suspect, too much reflection would hinder this process. Nevertheless, we guide these dreams using focus and feelings. Recognizing their emotional tags can help retrieve these dream memories. Like keywords, these tags let us find dream images that connect, and to separate those that don't.

Think of Stage 2 lucidity in terms more gentle than "directing" or "controlling." Meditate on an issue, scene, or emotion before going to sleep as a way of being better able to guide the consolidation of your memories in that direction. Put yourself into a state of mind, reaching toward pleasant, perplexed, wistful, lonely, reconciling, hopeful, thoughtful, or spiritual, to name a few.

> *"The first step in active imagination is to invite the creatures of the unconscious to come up to the surface and make contact with us."*
> — Robert Johnson, from *Inner Work*.

Consonance is important. When I am in turmoil, and desires are contrary to experience, I seem to have little vote in the dream experience. For example, if I'm engaged in a financial struggle in waking life in which I wish to succeed but if fears underlie that struggle, then fears will rule the night. Rather than trying to shotgun my way to success, I do better to reflect on the larger, positive lesson, or positive aspects of the experience. If I try to "surf" my emotional waves, I may have a chance to ride them into my subconscious.

Stage 3

Stage 3, slow-wave, non-REM sleep is our most dreamless. Our grogginess upon being awakened from Stage 3 indicates we were far from a thoughtful state. What was called Stage 4 sleep is now considered part of Stage 3. Even from this slow brainwave state far from the electrical signatures of consciousness, Matthew Walker tells us in *Why We Sleep*, there is a small chance of being woken to remember a dream.

The brain's glial cells shrink by 60% during Stage 3. These are the cells filling the space between neurons and which are four times more numerous than neurons. This amounts to a lot of shrinkage. With the shrinkage of the glial cells, the brain's cerebrospinal fluid can wash waste products out of the brain. It stands to reason that during this phase of sleep the primary goal is cleansing, not thinking.

> *"The brain only has limited energy at its disposal, and it appears that it must choose between two different functional states—awake and*

aware or asleep and cleaning up."
— Dr. Maiken Nedergaard, University of Rochester, Center for Translational Neuromedicine.

REM Sleep

Rapid Eye Movement sleep, or REM sleep, occurs over a handful of short discrete periods whose duration increases at the end of our night's sleep. REM sleep is considered the source of creativity. It seems our bodies attend to restoration and mental housekeeping before indulging in the creative license of REM sleep. Yet REM sleep is essential. People deprived of REM sleep for just a few days begin to show signs of psychotic behavior.

REM dreams are our most highly evolved dreams in both a neural and cognitive sense. They involve more of the prefrontal lobes than the other dream stages. They are cognitively complex in their use of pun, metaphor, allusion, allegory, contrast, symmetry, and other high-level concepts.

Reality-Checks

Lucidity in dreams first involves a recognition of oneself, and then exerting what appears as "will power" within the dream. It is suggested that reality-checks be used while dreaming to recognize when you're dreaming. To say to oneself, "This cannot be real. I must be dreaming!" Just to make this declaration appears to be an act of will, and thus a form of lucidity.

The idea behind reality-checks is embodied in the acronym ICE: "Intention, Clarity, Expectation." If you are in an expectant frame of mind—meaning you are expecting to become lucid—then the reality-check can establish that you're dreaming. With this clarity you can recover your intention to execute free will.

We have three different kinds of dream consciousness—present, reflective, and detached—which suggests three kinds of reality-checks. These develop somewhat from the different sleep states, although they can all occur within a REM-dream.

To develop the presence of mind to execute a reality-check from within a dream, it is suggested that we habituate ourselves to execute reality-checks in our waking state. I can report that my sensitivity to detail, and my awareness in general, have been amplified as the result of developing the habit of doing reality-checks in waking consciousness.

In a series of dreams, over several months, I repeatedly found myself leaping down flights of stairs. I might have once been able to do this in waking life, but I would not try it now—certainly not whole flights of stairs. In most cases, the experience was one of a controlled floating. Once I recognized that I could do this, I spent quite a bit of dreamtime floating down stairs. This was at the expense, I suspect, of whatever else I was in the dream to accomplish.

This was not lucidity in the sense of recognizing I was dreaming, but it was lucid to the degree that I took control of the dream, or had the impression that I did, and indulged in the pleasant sense of floating down stairways. One might argue that this was just the dream, and that could be the case, since these actions were symbolic. But this can always be argued no matter how lucid you think you are. The lack of intention and the presence of intention are both products of your imagination.

Lucid dreamers can execute actions they have agreed upon before sleeping, but their success varies. This means their lucidity varies.

Few people have demonstrated complete accuracy. One might ask, what is the benefit? The question of how lucid you want to be, and why, is not trivial. It is one you can ask of both your waking and sleeping self. Your answer may determine the level of lucidity you're able to achieve. Personally, I do not want to be too lucid, as I'm more interested in what my dreams can show me.

Awareness

Most dream discussions consider lucidity to be a single thing. It is many things and exists to many degrees. The nature of lucidity depends on the scope of your awareness at the time. For dogs, becoming lucid may be realizing that something is being asked of them; lucidity for dogs is realizing. If you're acting mindlessly, becoming lucid might mean coming back to your senses. If you're meditating, becoming lucid might mean the experience of a sense of contentment.

In dream work, opportunities to understand differ with your state of mind. Each potentially lucid state of mind offers you different senses of intention, clarity, and perspective.

Presence: experience, opportunity

Our normal waking state of presence is fairly absent. Our generally bored conscious mind sits at the gateway of our perception playing mental games of solitaire: worry, judgement, celebration or indulgence. While this is going on, we perceive reality like the boxes passing on a conveyor belt. As long as things fit a pattern, we don't question their reality, we just respond. It's a tennis-like "volley and serve;" it's fairly automatic. We can train ourselves to be more generally mindful, but if you look into the eyes of most people, they're not.

This is our normal REM dream state. Dream progress is linear, there is no reflection, no "subtle perception." If angels were speaking to most people, they would not hear them. To some extent, this is how our minds are supposed to be. We consider the perceptual input, categorize it, fit it into our world-model, and pick the optimal response. That your normal level of awareness in dreams mirrors your normal level of waking awareness is the starting point of dreamwork.

We get most of our paranormal reports from this state, I believe. When in this state, and when confronted with perceptions that don't fit, we are at a loss. Most people wall themselves off from the experience. If flashing lights descend upon us in the night, we lapse into confusion, prejudice, or disbelief. The dog growls, as does the dog part of our mind. A wiser person might say, "This is interesting; this is new… perhaps I'm dreaming. Let me test and find out." Or they might say, "I think this is a spirit trying to communicate. Let me investigate."

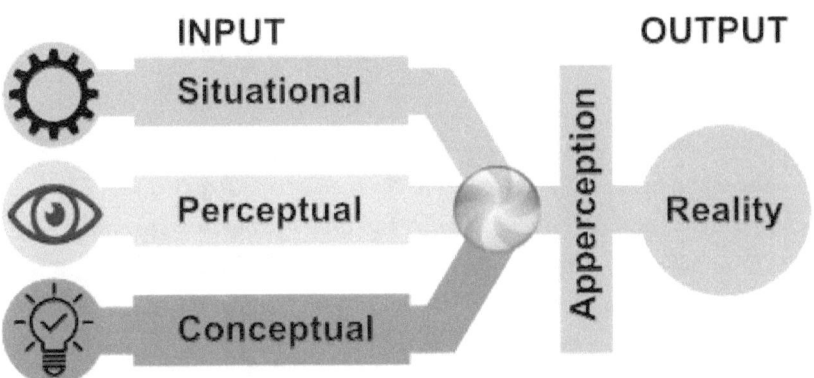

Reality-Check

You cannot ask anything without reflection; without reflection, your inner ability to ask questions is muted. Make your goal to reach reflection and once there to relax.

Practice relaxing in waking life. In a situation that would normally cause you to tense your body, loosen your body. In a situation that would normally cause you to focus more narrowly, focus more broadly.

When unusual situations occur, step back and take them in. Slow down, look around, sense your feelings. Stop what you're doing for a moment, become more attentive. Imagine you hear a single word where none has been spoken. If nothing comes, then give yourself that moment of mental silence in which something could. Perceive things from a different angle.

Reflection: thinking, creation of opportunity

Reflection means becoming aware of past and future, sense of choice, self-identification, cause, effect, and free will. This is naïve lucidity, a lucidity in which you believe yourself to be independent in your choices, and subject to things over which you have incidental control.

> *"For dreamers to become lucid while asleep, they must see past the overwhelming reality of their dream state, and recognize that they are dreaming. The same cognitive ability was found to be demonstrated while awake by a person's ability to think in a different way when it comes to solving problems."*
>
> — Patrick Bourke (2014). "Spontaneous Lucid Dreaming and Waking Insight", in *Dreaming*, Vol. 24 (2).

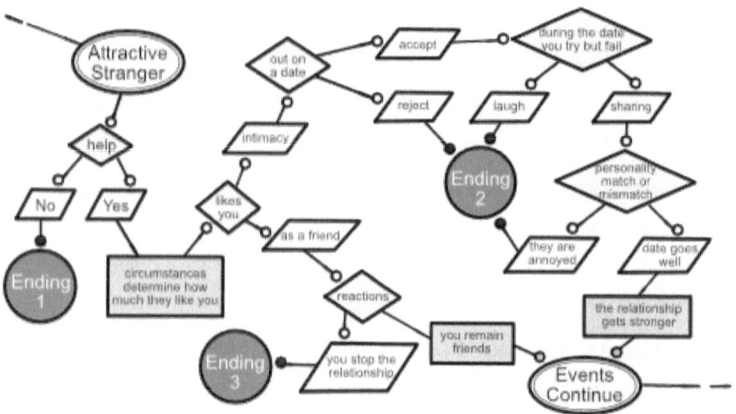

A narrative's cause-and-effect flow is a reflective thought structure.

Reality-Check

Ask yourself, what's logical? Ask yourself, what is meant within the container of what was said? Understand that most of what you perceive is what you expect to perceive. And that's okay, it's just a small selection of what's possible.

Being Lucid

We interpret what we see as making sense, even though everyday events are often illogical. We interpret what's going on around us as intentional, even though most of what we do is automatic and done without reflection.

Ask yourself, what are other people thinking? From their presentation, imagine what they're feeling. When you get a chance, stop what you're doing and ask what you are thinking. Touch base with your feelings.

Whenever your logic, intention, thinking, or feeling is unusual, ask yourself, is what you're seeing really there? Are you dreaming it up in waking life? Recognize that if you were dreaming, you'd believe anything... or almost anything.

You don't have to believe in reality entirely. If you find that you're surprised with your power, ability, or what's happening around you, then just acknowledge this power, ability, or event. How does it feel? How might you use it? What are you trying to achieve? How much of your limitations are in your mind?

Detachment: self-exploration, creation of thinking

> *"Every time I look deeply into someone's eyes, my consciousness is raised, as I register the other person's awareness and this moment of connection. Each time I see something unexpected, like a child's glove floating in a puddle like a starfish, my awareness clicks up a notch and I ask myself if I'm dreaming."*
>
> — Clare Johnson, from *Llewellyn's Complete Book of Lucid Dreaming*.

Detachment is the realm of deep mindfulness. Here is where you reflect on your ability to consider your situation, or to consider anything at all. In a state of detachment, you are more aware of creating perception, you have a greater awareness of attachments and the relative nature of your "free will." Detachment is a form of dissociation, a release of who you are so that you might become something else. This is reflective lucidity.

> *"Our results reveal shared neural systems between lucid dreaming and metacognitive function, in particular in the domain of thought monitoring."*
> — Elisa Filevich, Martin Dresler, Timothy R. Brick and Simone Kühn, (2015). "Metacognitive Mechanisms Underlying Lucid Dreaming," in *The Journal of Neuroscience,* Vol. 35 (3).

Recognize the subtle difference between feeling and emotion, such as exists between pain and suffering or between pleasure and happiness. In this space, you have inner free will. Free will to control how you will react to your experience. We use this in hypnotherapy to ease chronic pain, change habitual patterns, and develop new abilities. You can learn to hypnotize yourself to achieve these same effects.

Feelings strike like wind, and it often seems we're not prepared for them. They usually carry us off into a mood, even if we don't immediately act on them. This is a measure of our lack of being grounded. We are not equally grounded in all emotions.

In an attempt to disentangle our language, researchers are separating the ideas of feeling, mood, emotion, and emotional schema. Here is how I understand these things.

A feeling consists of the sense we have of ourselves at the moment along with the associations that sense elicits. Homesickness, melancholy, affection, irritation all have an immediate sense and a constellation of related thoughts.

A mood is a filter, or a shade that colors what we perceive. A mood has a feeling aspect, as I've just described, but it's importance lies in how it colors future events. Moods are the shepherds that direct our feelings.

An emotion is a basic thing; something we can categorize. We know what they are: anger, love, jealousy, fear, joy, contentment, and many others. We think we have some control over them, and that everyone experiences them in the same way. Neither are strictly true, and in many cases they are not true at all. An increasing number of researchers are coming to the conclusion that most of us do not, in fact, act reasonably but, instead, act emotionally.

> *"Many psychological scientists now assume that emotions are the dominant driver of most meaningful decisions in life."*
> — Jennifer Lerner, Ye Li, Piercarlo Valdesolo, and Karim Kassam, (2015). "Emotion and Decision Making," in *Annual Review of Psychology*. Vol. 66.

Emotional schemas are the ways we configure our behavior to express the emotions that underlie our feelings. Schemas differ between cultures and depend upon our moods.

The term alexithymia refers to a person's inability to express emotions or their inability to understand the emotions of others. Some people don't express emotions at all: think of Star Trek's Doctor Spock, or Conan Doyle's Sherlock Holmes.

Reality-Check

When you recognize a glitch in how you sense the world, give yourself a moment and consider these things: mood, feeling, emotion, and schema. We experience a glitch when one or more of these aspects is in conflict with our sense of reason. Don't rush into "doing" anything about it, just give yourself space. "Doing" is the reasonable reaction which won't settle these other aspects of yourself which are less localized in the moment.

Intention: opportunity, creation of experience

It's important to decide what you'd like to do, or to experience, when you become lucid in a dream. It's important to evoke the feeling. Simply saying "I want to have a lucid dream," is a concept that lacks feeling. What do you want to feel? What emotion will bring you there?

Lie quietly, before going to sleep, and visualize the experience that you want to have in your dream. This is not to make the images habitual, as the images will be forgotten but to evoke the emotions. The emotions you draw on will resonate with deeper needs and pervasive feelings. These emotions will shape the geography of your dreams.

> *"When you are in the inner world, everything seems to be based on feelings. In order to fly, you need the feeling of flying... and then you fly."*
>
> — Jerimiah Molfese, from *My Adventures in Lucid Dreaming*.

What arrives is open to your judgement but not your control. In this mature lucidity, you have greater awareness. An essential part of this is the awareness that you are not making this up. You are inviting it, not inventing it. That being said, you can also dis-invite it.

"One precaution must be observed: once you have found the image and started the inner dialog, you must relinquish control," says

Robert Johnson. He does not say, but he should say, that you absolutely retain the right to protect yourself. This is a most important caution: do not conjure any energy more powerful than yourself, unless you trust it absolutely. To do otherwise is dangerous to your health, and the health of others, as these energies can possess you.

Reality-Check

Reason gives rise to intention and emotion gives rise to inclination. Reason and emotion exist in us to create a feedback loop: the first informs the second, which informs the first, which informs the second, and so on. We are in synchrony with ourselves when this process converges and the whole thing settles down.

We like it when things settle down, when we feel resolved, but resolution should be recognized as more of a feeling than a judgement. It is good to experience these two systems informing each other. Developing a tolerance to observe their dislocation without becoming distressed is a good thing. Sometimes conflict exists in ways you cannot resolve, and you would do well to recognize and accept the reality of it, even if you don't want to.

There is always a "middle way" within a conflict, which may be the best way, or the best way for the moment, but it is often fragile and weakly supported. Being quick to embrace a resolution can be headstrong and inconsiderate. Consider being more considerate and less headstrong, if only to see what opportunities it provides.

Metacognitive Illusions

These optical illusions illustrate how we create our visual reality. They make us think we are seeing something that is not there. Watch how you react when perception conflicts with expectation.

Becoming Lucid

To what degree do you question the thing you're looking at, and to what degree do you question yourself and your self-awareness? If this were taking place in a dream, it would be an opportunity to become lucid.

- How much of what is there are you seeing? And how much of what you're seeing is there?
- How much of what is true are you aware of? And how much of what you're aware of is true?

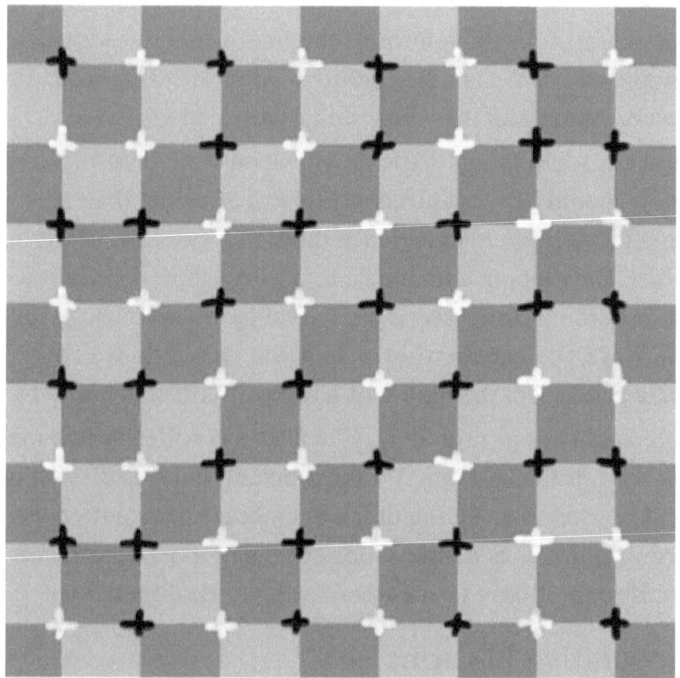

Wiggling Rectangle

Being Lucid

Scintillating dots

Rotating Squares

Pre-lucidity Example: Connecting with the Dream

This morning I had a dream, and in the dream I was preparing for a journey. I had made some resolutions, and I fulfilled some resolutions. I spent some time with people, most of whom I didn't know, and one I did. I marveled at how boring and uninteresting most of them were and wondered why I, and the one friend I knew in the group, put up with them all. I had resolved to return to visit an old friend before he died, and I had done that. There was a feeling of things being packed and organized. Then, gradually, I woke up.

Upon waking, I reflected on the feelings in my body and what things lay in the day ahead. I felt a combination of soreness and moving electrical energy, a result from having been out running the day before. I had not yet opened my eyes.

My first thought was to leave behind the physical feelings, and transition into the mentality of the day ahead. My second thought was to tell myself—addressing a sort of imaginary collective of myself—"Everyone with electrical sensations should remain in bed, with their eyes closed, and consider how these sensations correspond to future events." I relaxed back into my body and luxuriated in sensations. At the same time I hazily cogitated about the dawning of a busy day.

I cultivated the hypnopompic state. "Making sense" is distorted in that state. I lay there feeling the coursing of bodily sensations, along with the experience of thinking about thinking, without really doing it. I thought about all the doings of things without focusing on the things that were to be done. I connected the doing of things with the sensations in my body.

The result was not any thoughts or memories at all, just a sense of connection, and the overall feeling that whatever tasks were to be done in the coming day were settled in the body, and the body was relaxed about them.

Pre-lucidity Exercise:
Weaving the Subconscious into the Conscious

This exercise is to be done upon first rising to waking consciousness, before you open your eyes, start thinking, or get out of bed. This is the hypnopompic state, and the exercise is to retain that state for as long as possible.

Upon waking, begin recalling your dreams. If they are not clear as such, then collect your memories from the night as fleeting images, and gather a few. Scan these few images or feelings. They may not seem like dream elements but, if they are recent memories, they might not connect to events in your waking life, either. Line up these three or four memories like Easter Eggs, without pressing them into any linear form or causal sequence. Give each a name or word to help you remember them.

Observe your body as you are lying in bed with eyes closed. Explore how your body feels. Move your body slightly, if you need some stimulation or sensation. You can flex your muscles without changing position. Focus on three or four parts of your body and place them in association with the memory fragments you have named. There is no need to make sense of this. If you're in a proper hypnopompic state with your normal cogitating thoughts disengaged, this should seem entirely natural.

Take each name, word, image, mood, or recalled sensation and associate it with some part of your physical body. Sit with this for a moment and reflect on how it feels. You'll have a variety of fleeting feelings.

Becoming Lucid

After a minute or two, your waking mind will come "online," and it—that is you—may become impatient with remaining in the background. Let wakefulness emerge, so that you become more verbal and lucid. As this happens, reflect on the illogic of this exercise, and you may forget what you've done. Whatever you do is fine. Just watch the process of emergence from being asleep to being awake, and your own actions in connecting the two.

> " 'Ought to 'ave some testimonials,' said Sir Ector doubtfully. 'It's usual.'
>
> 'Testimonials!' said Merlyn, holding out his hand. Instantly, there were some heavy tablets in it signed by Aristotle, a parchment signed by Hecate, and some type written duplicates signed by the Master of Trinity, who could not remember having met him...
>
> ' He 'ad 'em up 'is sleeve...' said Sir Ector wisely.
>
> 'Tree!' said Merlyn. At once, there was an enormous mulberry growing in the middle of the courtyard, with its luscious fruits ready to patter down...
>
> 'Hay do it with mirrors,' said Sir Ector.
>
> 'Snow!' said Merlyn, '... and an umbrella,' he added hastily. Before they could turn around, the copper sky of summer had assumed a cold and lowering bronze, while the biggest white flakes that were ever seen were floating about them and settling on the battlements. An inch of snow had fallen before they could speak, and all were trembling before the wintry blast...
>
> 'It's done by 'ipnotism,' said Sir Ector with chattering teeth. 'Like 'os wallahs from the Indies... but that'll do,' he added hastily. 'That'll do

very well.'"
— T. H. White, from *The Once and Future King*.

"*Self-reflection in everyday life is more pronounced in persons who can easily control their dreams.*"
— Elisa Filevich, (2015). "Metacognitive Mechanisms Underlying Lucid Dreaming", in *The Journal of Neuroscience*, Vol. 35 (3).

Hypnotic Session 4

Mindscape audio file at:
https://www.mindstrengthbalance.com/becoming-lucid-audio/

Mindscape

Let's count down to a simple state of almost sleeping mind. To be as calm and quiet as possible, being awake only to hear my voice, with disengaged thoughts just idling past. Place your feet on the floor, your hands on your thighs or your lap as we start. Be relaxed and aware.

Use your imagination to picture yourself approaching a beach that's in the distance. Evoke the strongest memory senses you have: the sights of the beach, the feel of the sand, the salt air, the sounds of the beach, the birds, the rumble of waves, and the hiss of sand.

Allow me to create a sense of presence for you, as I speak this journey. Full of detail, felt through memories and associations. Imagination is remembering: start with the image, sound, or feeling. Get the image and stabilize it. Keep hold of it, draw it out, and call up more images, sounds, and feelings.

Imagine you're approaching this beach; it's summer in the evening. Build a picture from fragments—looking out to the horizon, looking up to the sky, looking back to the woods—and wrap this around you like a movie screen. Transport yourself into the movie. Now we'll take three deep breaths...

One... into the rich air of the night, and exhale as the edges of the screen disappear behind you... Two... a damp breeze caresses your right forearm. The air brushes your forehead...

And Three... the sounds of water, birds, waves on the beach, and the deep distance.

Once the feeling is stable, you don't need to watch it. As we all learn, what we see remains intact even when we close our eyes. The sun has set. The last day's light lingers on an indigo horizon. You are walking down a darkening path through a wide and open wood.

See the waves breaking beyond the trees, the shore approaching. In front and below, growing around you, is a wide bay... with a beach... with driftwood at the tide line and gravel down to a small, gentle surf.

Close your eyes now, and imagine you are looking up into a dark sky sprinkled with stars growing like a sound, rising like a tide, rotating like a spinning ball, above a sea draped over the horizon.

Let your mind rest, your thoughts quiet. You've stopped moving and stand comfortably overlooking the black painted sea, velvet sky pinned with stars and sand dust.

Place your attention in your hands. Let your hands vibrate with the shimmer of the stars.

Take a breath... pause, and exhale with the slow sweep of the sky. Take a second breath... inhale the smell of the ocean, and the jeweled sky comes closer, clearer, surrounding you completely.

We'll explore three states of mind. States of mind we have all the time—layered and sandwiched together, complementing each other. States always so much in front of us that we don't notice they're separate, or even there, in front of us, coloring our experience from the prosaic, profane, attentive, immediate, spiritual, circumspect, somnolent, celebratory, and back again to a detached state.

The first thought-form is presence; just being, just watching. We observe, we act, we respond. The world comes to us, immediate and sensory. Relax your thoughts and feel your presence now, on this beach, in your imagination.

Is it real? As real as it ever is. Accept it completely as instantly authentic as any memory can be. If you notice your attention drawn away, let it snap-back. Present here, now, and always. With no past, no history, and no plans or future. Just be here, watching, accepting, experiencing.

Presence is focus on the moment, listening for details below hearing, motions caught on the tail end, facial expressions barely lasting a microsecond. Presence is what we always have, to fleeting degrees, with moments of attention and moments of distraction. Like a thought, presence comes with the asking and dissolves a moment later. The waves roll. The birds call. Take a breath... relax. You watch, you feel, and you experience...

Now, as you're watching, from your left, a glowing sphere appears. A silent, white, glowing ball moving from left to right. Fuzzy in its outline. Slower than a bird, faster than a balloon.

Just watch, accept, and experience as it moves over the beach, gliding over the sand, not touching, featureless. There it is, not to be questioned, moving left to right, blown by a wind that isn't there. It moves across your field of vision, amazing in its appearance, coming from nowhere with no explanation. It moves past, leaving behind a thermal wake, a silent siren that would drop in tone, if it had any tone to start with.

You turn to the right, and it seems to slow, shrinking into the distance, fading to invisible. Take a breath… and let it go, as if it was never there in the first place. It's gone, and we don't think about it… anymore. Be present.

To be lucid in presence is to become aware. Subtle perception is awareness of changes in your peripheral fields… background images, sounds, feelings. Shades of what you're normally unaware of. Shapes of darkness and sounds of silence. Fine lines traced over clear images, murmurs behind sounds clearly heard. Be open, aware, and attuned.

As all of this is going on, there is a second thought-form, always on the sideline, and this second thought-form is reflection. Like the crackling in a glaze. The scratches on a glass pane that pop out when light glances at an angle. Reflection is a sense of self, a sense of difference, a sense of standing behind yourself, standing behind the person who is watching.

There is the thing that we are watching, and there is us. You are separate, you are thoughtful, you are conscious. Reflection says, "What do I look like? What am I doing here?" And the answer comes, "You're thinking a thought. Creating an image. Building a reality out of memories."

Take a breath, and let it fill your chest, extend out through your body, respirating, holding, expanding, and defining. Exhale, separate, the air that is not you. Still in your identity. Watching, thinking, always reflecting on what, and why, and where, and when. What's happening and why?

Reflection is the awareness of your role in manufacturing your presence. Reflection is to recognize that if you closed your eyes and ears, and let drift your connection that you maintain through force of will, then you would not be present anymore. Reflection is to recognize that it is you who is holding yourself above the ocean of absence. How balanced are you? How complete are you? Is there more balance to be found, more to complete?

We're always turning to face the future, escaping before us like a chased rabbit, never catching it. It defines us, leaning always into the future like walkers into a heavy wind. Take a breath, inhale... lean from the past into your future-self. Relax and hang in limbo. Exhale, falling around an orbit, forever falling over a future horizon.

Reflective lucidity is watching thoughts form. Holding imaginal images steady. It's the whirling of the dervish, spinning and stately, thinking experience and feeling perception. Watching thoughts bubble up like waters in a spring, mix and mingle, proclaim their independence and disappear downstream.

Move to the third thought-form—the thought-form of detachment. Recognizing the process of processing perception. The process of assembling the thoughts about what we perceive. It's a hesitation, a small suspicion that things might be different. An unpackaging to note that what you see is what you've chosen

Being Lucid

to see. It's a fragile process, and we're not adept at it. As the most thoughtful of processes, we do it best when we don't think about it.

Your presence is your construction, a choice of one among many, from necessity, convenience, or just habit. Maybe not quite so necessary; maybe not the most convenient; maybe not even your own habit but built by those around you, whose needs, preferences, and habits might not be right, best, or even real.

The consensus illusion is the half-light we all agree to accept as normal. Busy, as you are, experiencing it as real and immediate, busy building your own past, constantly inflating your self-identity, like blowing into a leaking air mattress, floating on the social ocean, fabricating your future on the best guess of the present.

We are not yet evolved to think too long about the lion our perception tells us is real, lest it eat us. Yet to elevate ourselves above our lot requires a realization of alternatives. Was it fate, chance, expected outcome, or accident? Lift up the edges of perception. To what is your sense of self attached? Might there be another reality that you might join, or see, or be? Who decides and how? The greatest power comes from recognizing that it was you who built it.

And now the glowing orb comes for its last pass, again riding the wind, bouncing off the black sand to be carried rightward with the power of the wind. Maybe it isn't real, or maybe it's more real. Maybe you can call it to you, or extinguish it entirely. With a burst of novelty, the orb shoots upward as if deflected.

Tip back your head to see it shooting into the sky, a shooting star that you've created. An element of reality you control.

Now, blow the whole thing up.

Let the beach silently explode, in a volcano of confetti and star flakes, sucked into the drain-hole of a reality whose plug you've pulled. Break it into fragments and see it all vacuumed up, like a gravitational Big Crunch, to disappear into a Black Hole that only gets smaller and smaller... the more it engorges. Until there's nothing left but the quiet of blue space... and a few lines of tape, on a stage. Tape that marks the positions where things were placed. And your reality oscillates between the empty and the waiting, the absent, and the everything.

Lucidity in detachment is to detach again, from whatever you detached into. Let loose your perception and descend in the safety of a bathyscaphe into the void. Start over to see behind the history, the raw potential of having any thoughts at all. Don't hold onto any of it. Just to remember the whole without naming any of the parts. Just to remember a sense of awe.

The first level is to watch the game. The second level is to play the game. The third level is to make the game. And we do these all the time, all at once, with shifting attentions and awareness. Dreams layer the alternatives. The witness, the engagement, the construction. We witness the alternatives, alternatives we might construct, and how self and otherness are constrained and might be different.

Go bigger now, to have the sense of self in jumbled thought-forms. To start again, to watch the game of chaos, witness, and fabrication. And let it shift, sift, boil, bubble, disintegrate, evaporate, blow like ashes from a campfire.

Let these visions fade, like fading dreams, transporting you back to presence. Bring up the house lights into the present, the stern reality of now. Coming back, returning to the room, the role, the familiar script, spoken in your own voice. Always watched, played, and constructed.

Take a breath, define your bones, your skin, your energy. Three... two... one... ** snap **. Carefully open your eyes, so as not to lose your balance, as you slip back into yourself. Present, calm, clear, and comfortable. Wide awake. You're back. We're done.

5 Waking Lucidity

"The purpose of active imagination is not to 'program' the unconscious, but to listen to the unconscious. And, if you do, the unconscious, in turn, will listen to you."
— Robert Johnson, from *Inner Work: Using Dreams and Active Imagination for Personal Growth*.

We spend most of our time in a state of nonreflective awareness, receiving perceptions without judgement. This pre-primate, in-the-moment state is supported by our parietal and central brain structures, which we share with other mammals. From this awareness, we perceive the external world as dominated by events. We perceive an internal world dominated by emotions. Our nonreflective state operates with little sense of extension in time or deduction. The guiding senses of awareness operating here are memory, symbolic inference, and association—call this our instinctive mind.

Our uniquely primate prefrontal cortex rides shotgun over unfolding affairs. It generates an incessant chatter that serves to orient us and whose verbiage is quickly forgotten. This dissociated awareness acts as analyst, editor, narrator, director, secretary, bouncer, creator, judge, and agent. Our prefrontal awareness is weakly connected to our emotions. It generates a solipsistic sense of truth, and therefore a selfish sense of advantage. This higher level of self-awareness is the agent of premeditated creative and destructive acts.

The majority of time our analytical mind churns out a kind of thought-foam making a mud of incidental perceptions and reflections. From this mud there emerges our situational awareness, and with this mud we broadcast our position to others. This thought-foam becomes the substrate of social bonding and consensus reality. Its self-direction is weak, and its novelty is marginal.

The pollution of this thought foam with unproductive, conflicting, or destructive ideas can undermine the positive potential of our social efforts, which is to say, our collective effect on our environment and each other. This judgement is only valid relative to a larger perspective.

Our instinctive and analytical minds are in weak connection—the analytical mind being somewhat aware of, but not particularly responsive to, our instinctive mind. Our instinctive mind, on the other hand, is barely aware of, or responsive to, our ratiocinations.

It is incorrect to call these our conscious and subconscious minds. Both operate together and it is their combined action that supports awareness. It is more true to say our analytical mind dominates waking awareness like the driver of a horse and buggy. Our body, being the buggy and the horse, being our instinctive mind. Our instinctive mind dominates normal dreaming, where perception is drawn solely from memory. We can change this balance through meditation and lucid dreaming.

Waking Practice

The purpose of the Waking Practice Exercises is to become habituated to lucid thinking in our daily lives. Judging from brain scans and the reports of lucid dreamers, our normal waking state is a combination of the previously mentioned, two levels of awareness which reflect our evolution.

The purpose of these exercises is to strengthen the connection between these two modes of awareness. To develop habits of thought that connect analysis with instinct, presence with difference, and discernment with confabulation. There, it seems, lies our evolution.

Exercises

— **Waking Exercise #1**: Periodically, throughout your day, ask yourself, "What is there in front of me that I have not seen before?"

— **Waking Exercise #2**: Make it a regular practice to tell yourself, "I am dreaming; I am experiencing the world as a dream. The people around me are dreaming. I can stop. I can think of myself separate from this dream."

— **Waking Exercise #3**: When you are struck by certain observations, either incidental or familiar, ask yourself, "What feelings are being evoked that I might explore, which I have not explored before? What might I become more awake to?"

— **Waking Exercise #4**: At various points throughout your day, ask yourself, "Where was I at this time yesterday? How did I feel at that time? Where will I be at this time tomorrow?"

— **Waking Exercise #5**: Throughout your day, when your attention is drawn to a particular person, object, or action ask yourself, "If I could have an effect on this person, object, or action, what would that be?" Say clearly to yourself what you would like to do or to have happen. Visualize this happening in your mind. Then let it go and return to "normal."

— **Waking Exercise #6**: At occasional points in your day, ask yourself, "What are the true feelings of this landscape in which I find myself?"

"Just as one can compose colors or forms, so one can compose (e)motions."

— adapted from Alexander Calder, painter, sculptor, and designer (1898-1976).

Hypnotic Session 5

Being Awake audio file at:
https://www.mindstrengthbalance.com/becoming-lucid-audio/

Being Awake

Relax into a comfortable position. Quiet your movements. Quiet your thoughts. Listen to my voice and the messages coming from your body. For the duration of this exercise you won't need to pay attention to anyone. Remain alert but have no interest in the talk inside your head. Let your mind keep talking, or mumbling, or calling out, but as if from another room. You can close the door.

Drift into the light, middle zone of trance. As if you were a dried flower, perfectly balanced, intact, and motionless. Let time slow down and stop. Pencils balance motionless on their points. Flower petals hang suspended in midair. The world hardly affects you.

I want you to turn off your verbal mind and in its place, focus on the sounds and images that you create. This is just like watching a movie, except that the movie is in your mind, and you're not judging it. No more thinking about thinking, so forget about the reality-TV of your mind. For the time of this exercise, accept whatever you see, or imagine as being real, reflecting what's real, or reflecting what's inside you.

Step inside my elevator of awareness, a spacious window-filled ship with comfortable seats. Take a breath and feel the bones in your arms shudder to relax, shake off their jittery plaque, and your arms feel heavy… Take another breath into your legs, and the bones in your legs relax. First, they jitter and shake, and then they subside and they too feel heavy. Feel the heaviness and warmth in your arms and legs. So heavy. As if all their muscles relaxed, those muscles attaching them to you… relaxed. And begin to float in your imagination.

Now you are walking through an urban landscape. Imagine a wide promenade, a walk paved with flagstones, lined with planters with red and white petaled flowers, bushes with light leaves, dark leaves, and red leaves. You are walking between two buildings, following a path you've walked before. Put yourself inside this picture, attending to your footing, the path, and the high windowed valley walls on either side.

Ask yourself, "What is there in front of me that I have not seen before?" And here the answer is everything. Everywhere you cast your eye, you're creating as you go like taking a cloth to wipe condensation off a window, revealing the landscape beyond.

You look up to the building on the left and notice bevels on the window frames, black gutters on the roof edge, yellow trim against the grey wall. It's a rich grey, richer than you recall, with tones of blue. The yellow seems sharp against a powder blue sky. Close your mind's eye and see the after image: white walls traced with blue lines against a yellow sky.

What is in front of you that you have not seen before? Your footsteps, the patterns in the pavement, the echo that changes as the walls change shape. Temperature that changes to warm above the flagstone, cool shadows, moist vegetation. What have you not felt before? Is it changes in light? Breathe the air. Is it thicker or thinner, richer or leaner, thinner or fatter?

Fasten your point of view to a wall, a tree, or a tripod, as if you're looking through the viewfinder of a camera. Step away from the camera, but continue to see through the eye of the camera and easily walk into your own field of view. Watch yourself slowly walk away. And how strange it is to see yourself walking away from yourself. What do you look like? Would you recognize yourself? Would you be surprised?

Now you're in a diner, a restaurant you know from memory. You really were there once, as you can recall. Maybe, it's evening and the sky is getting dark or maybe, it's early morning and there is filtered overcast.

There are many tables, each with their own lights. There are many people, you can see their faces. You know you're dreaming, and you say to yourself, "This is a dream. These people I have imagined. They're part of the dream, too." And so it is in waking life where so much rests on memory. Memories of how people behave, what their signals mean, our intentions, and how we create our social space. That too is made up, assumed, and projected. So, we're all dreaming, and we can stop dreaming and recollect ourselves.

As you look around, in this restaurant of your memory, say to yourself, "I can be in the present without that cloud of pretense and preconception. I can be awake among others who are asleep. I can observe the finest details without having to know, interpret, or evaluate everything. I can sense subtle changes without explanations white-washing my perception."

You will recall this later today, when you're out of your house, in the street, behind the wheel, or in the countryside. How much there is to sense without knowing, see without distinguishing, and hear without classifying. You watch yourself watching, aware of your mind's eye roving from one thing to the next... and the next.

Now you're walking through a wood, groomed and manicured like a park. Meandering paths bordered by close-cropped bushes. Tall fir trees rise like temple columns to a woven green roof above. Twigs and leaflets intertwine and interlace. Trees with their own unique and separate beings which, to you, are part of the woodwork.

And you are struck by the thought of how much passes you unnoticed. There is a whole biosystem, a tree-top ecosystem inhabited by flocks of birds, that seems like nothing but a ceiling to you. There are chemistries of earth and air and communications vibratory, auditory, and olfactory that you can't sense. What would it feel like to be over the landscape rather than under the tree tops? In the earth and not on it or living in the air?

Ask yourself, "What other perspectives might I have overlooked or under-looked?" Are there feelings that you could have, right now, that you don't have, because of some barely justified reason to feel otherwise? Ask yourself, "What feelings are being evoked that I might explore, which I have not explored before? What might I become more awake to?"

Can you recall where you were yesterday at this time? Can you recall what you thought yesterday at this time? Can you recall how you felt yesterday at this time? Tell yourself, "I will feel good now, today, at this time, and tomorrow I will remember that I did." As you get hungry or sleepy, on a certain cycle, tell yourself that you'll try getting happy, curious, or thoughtful with some certain regularity, so that you might know you did, and what you felt and the results of what you saw because of it.

Make that resolution now, that at some time of day, each day, you'll reach into your closet of emotions and try on a few like a person might consider their umbrella while looking at a sky of unsettled weather.

Now you are at your doorway, and you're stepping out, and you see the clouds are broken. And the clouds are bright, and the sky is blue, and the air is clear, and the weather is good. And you wonder how patterns around you—in the people you see, the seasons you weather, and the landscape you travel—affect the moods that come and go.

Ask yourself, "What are the true feelings of this landscape?" Ask yourself, "Is my mood my own, or am I carrying some mood that I picked up like a stain on my coat, a burr on my sleeve, or a stick in my shoe?" What other moods might you have, and what directs you to the mood you're in? Could you listen to moods the way your listen to traffic... or the wind? Could you sense and navigate among moods like obstacles on your course? Why adopt one, when you could chose another? Ask yourself, "Am I in the right mood now and if I stop, settle, and give myself more space, might new moods come that I don't usually have time for?"

Settle into your mood, and feel it start to drift, or blow, or wash away. Let the thoughts and words cease—spoken or heard, muttered or grumbled. It's quiet now, and all you have is feeling, like the heavy and relaxed feeling you created, and there are other feelings, in your body, in your bones, in the air around you. Can you clear the space of all feelings, and how would that feel? Can you have an emotion without a feeling? Can you have an emotion without those feelings that you associate with it?

Try experiencing calm, centered, relaxation without any feeling. Disconnect from all sensation, internal and external, and see if you can be filled with peace, or confidence, or love, or energy, or curiosity. And relax again.

Take a breath... and let it out... and come back to feeling nothing. Just presence as empty as possible. Unattached to all the thoughts, feelings, and emotions that swirl around you much of the time. And say to yourself, "I like the quiet. I like the choice. I like the space to grow."

And in your day, the hours ahead, the days ahead, when you take note of things happening around you, and you notice something in particular or someone doing something that catches your attention—perhaps they engage you, or they repel you, or they attract you—you'll stop shrinking them in a narrowing focus... and instead unwrap more space and enlarge them.

When you see something unusual—or someone who catches your eye, or ear to cause that short hesitation of an unexpected thought—you'll take that thought, plucked like a flower, or picked like a fruit, and you'll examine it. And you'll ask yourself, "What is this thought, feeling, or emotion, and is it mine or is it manufactured?" And you'll ask yourself, "What thought might I have, or feeling grasp, or emotion create for myself, or adopt from somewhere around me? And do I want that thought? Do I want to amplify or diminish it before passing it on?"

See your thoughts, feelings, and emotions as shared things like the air we breathe, that we change in its chemistry and then pass on. And what do you want to put into this air you're leaving behind? And what do you want to accept from this air you're inhaling? What if other people's thoughts, feelings, and emotions left trails of scent that we pick up without knowing?

And what if these are dream-thoughts you're having? And what might be the thoughts that other people are having, and are they dreaming too? And ask yourself, "How might things be otherwise?" And listen... listen to the quiet around you, and hear it full of noises, echoes, and reflections of things near and far, outside and inside you. And settle that all down to a zero that's not a nothing, just the average baseline, the average noise of sound, and thought, and emotion. That zero baseline out of which everything materializes, and you call it quiet.

Hear the quiet and relax. Feel the heavy weight in your arms and your legs. Sense yourself sitting comfortably, calm, and clear-headed. All you feel now is your sense of self. Your emotion is alert, curious, and positive. With some excitement you look upon what new thoughts, feelings, and emotions you will create as if from a new perspective, as if flying over the forest of feelings, rather than being below and beneath it.

To glide through a wide blue sky of possibilities. To soar on thermals, lifted like bubbles of emotion, avoiding some, engaging others. To master flight through thoughts and feelings, no longer limited to scrabble over rough terrain.

Relax. Take a breath... exhale... and return to the sleep of the waking mind, saddled, bridled, and hitched to the wagon of daily progress. Back to waking life, with all in order, hair combed, and collar straightened. Three... two... one. You're back and ready to open your eyes. Be here.

6 Hypnagogic Lucidity

"The more attention you pay to your dreams, the more they respond with brighter, more memorable, more interesting imagery."
— Clare Johnson, from *Llewellyn's Complete Book of Lucid Dreaming*.

Lucidity in dreaming follows lucidity in waking life. The more the two overlap, the more you will be able to move between them collaboratively.

Hypnagogia is a state that precedes falling asleep but comes to us fleetingly in other situations: trance, vacant stare, light hypnosis, waking amnesia, or a deep daydream. These states have a common dissociated feel, but the state preceding sleep, in my experience, has a uniquely relaxed flow. This is the state we'd like to enhance and explore.

Hypnagogia offers you the chance to orient yourself before entering the dream state. And while it may be true that you could sooner drive a camel through the eye of a needle than bring your riches into heaven that is sort of what you're doing here: you're bringing ego awareness into a state of oneness with the present. Don't bring the whole camel, you don't need it. As you fall asleep, hold only the essence of who you are, and how you feel. The dream-world is a thought-responsive environment.

Hypnagogic Practice

The practice of hypnagogic lucidity trains presence, patience, and stability during change. It is the latter—stability during change as well as creating change in the otherwise unaware dream-phase—that defines lucidity.

The key to retaining lucidity through hypnagogia is to remain present while being completely relaxed. Hypnagogia is a state of consciousness that can easily be lost. Do not move, shift your eyes, alter your attention, verbalize, or carry on any thoughts. Reside only in your feeling of self and your emotional state. Who you are and how you feel must remain calm, unobtrusive, and ever-present. Let the dream-state coalesce around your identity like the layers of a pearl. Of course, what you really should do is whatever feels natural in this situation. My instructions are only suggestions.

Exercises

— **Hypnagogic Exercise #1**: Clare Johnson lists six stages of hypnagogia. Create these stages to help you drop into a deeper state while retaining self-awareness. Memorize these six stages, and create them as you're falling asleep.

1. Clouds or waves of light or color: still feeling awake and hearing yourself think.

2. Initial lights: stars, sparks, or dots approaching, receding, or traversing your field of view.

3. Static, flat images: geometric shapes, faces, complexities you cannot recognize.

4. Transient 3D images: momentary flashes of depth of, at most, a few seconds duration.

5. 3D scenes without any sense of narrative. Witnessing dreamlike excerpts without feeling involved.

6. Full immersion. When the scene has a narrative, and you're in it, then you're dreaming.

— **Hypnagogic Exercise #2**: Follow body sensations. After you're comfortable, and the lights are out, sink into your body, and amplify your sensations. Focus on sounds and sensations on, around, and throughout your body. Recall feelings of things you've experienced —sun, water, motion, movement—and imagine yourself in those situations.

— **Hypnagogic Exercise #3**: Create a dream vision. Build a clear and detailed fantasy. Focus on feelings and allow unbidden feelings. Pay attention to your progression through the six stages of Exercise #1. Focus on keeping your sense of self undisturbed.

— **Hypnagogic Exercise #4**: The body scan. This is a form of progressive relaxation with the addition of retaining consciousness. Imagine a small warming ball of white light running over the surface of your skin. Create it at the crown of your head and move it around in circles that cover your scalp, and then encircle your head, traveling across your face, cheeks, and behind your head. Let this ball of light travel in a spiral pattern all the way down your body, down each arm to the fingers, and down each leg to the toes. Imagine, in as much detail as you can, the warm feeling of this energetic ball, as it slowly and evenly travels over your whole body.

One scan should take 15 minutes. If you start to doze off, return to a clear sense of self and your perception of this moving ball. Be alert for odd sounds and sensations.

"Why does the eye see a thing more clearly in dreams, than the imagination when awake?"
— Leonardo da Vinci, artist, engineer, scientist (1452-1519)

Hypnotic Session 6

Illuminations audio file at:
https://www.mindstrengthbalance.com/becoming-lucid-audio/

Illuminations

Make yourself comfortable. Imagine you have magic hands that you can hold away from your body, as your body reclines in a comfortable position. Imagine yourself outside your body, so that you're standing in front of yourself, and your hands are palms out, and you're facing your body. Through your hands, register the degree of comfort and relaxation of your body.

Draw your hands across the surface of your seated skin. Feel in your palms the pressures on your skin. Transfer back to your skin the lightness and warmth you feel surrounding your hands, so that your body is levitating, light, and comfortable.

Imagine yourself in the most comfortable place you could be. A place not only physically comfortable, but mentally and emotionally comfortable. Maybe it's somewhere you were as a child, or a feeling you had out of doors, or sense of being loved, whole, and essential. Let that feeling envelop you, surround and secure you, so that it is as strong now as it was then.

Relax and take a breath and with the breath, fill yourself with remembered comfort—deep comfort that is more than physical. Associate with that comfort a memory or sensation, as you exhale not from your lungs but from your memory, letting all sense of the present disperse into the air around you.

Hypnagogic Lucidity

Sense waves of color or light around you. Feel these colors shifting and changing shape. Sense the different feelings of the different colors. Reach out, and let these colored clouds blow through your fingers.

Look more closely for quick changes at the edges, static sparks or dots of color moving in the folds. Look to where the stars or dots are going or coming from. Create these twinklings at the edge of your field of vision. Give them energy, not as thoughts, but as attractors of attention. Imagine they are the firings of nerves, the conception of ideas, or the connections between thoughts. Imagine bits of yourself in these sparks.

Let wreaths of images unroll around you, boundaries of your space, textures, or tracings. Blink your mind to see their hanging afterimages: geometric shapes, vines, and curlicues. Patterns, raised relief, grooves, folds, and crisp lines running through the clouds, over hills, fields, and forests of your imagination.

As these forests grow, give them time, and space to fill, rooting in the fertile openness of your mind, not holding onto thoughts, but letting thoughts come and go, to be blown to pieces, dissolving into other thoughts and associations.

As if you are some old celluloid projector, see motion flicker in your images, figures changing their pose, sky clouds rolling, or breaking ocean waves. Let spray wet your awareness like the wave tongues that catch your feet, tidal swells floating life into ideas and fading with each passing.

Wait, and watch, and witness as ideas grow, like dialogs auditioned, statements coming from nowhere, passing by. A snatch of dialog, perhaps inaudible, indistinct, words spoken by someone, conversations from across the room, dimmed by distance.

Focus on them more. Focus on the sounds and associations that fur your memories. Build your memories from the outside in like chocolates soft at the center, sweet with presence, warm with emotion. You are watching, in a café, a social gathering, many stalls with conversations in fits and starts.

Focus on each with their similar textures, and reflect on how there is too much talking and not enough saying. Fill in a thick impasto, spread with a painting-knife, a hair thin spatula. Brushed, burnished, glistening, glossy, moving with inner light, painted with a thick oiled memory in Titanium White, Ochre, Cerulean, Cadmium, Crimson, or Ultramarine.

Listen for the sounds, memories of sounds, drifting from other alcoves in your brain. Drums covered with metal, plastic, wood, or fabric. Soft vowels, sharp consonants, squeaking hinges, susurrating slippers, and whispering winds... rustling, murmuring. A snapping twig, an acorn on a tin roof, rain driven on an old window.

Pick a place to be and feel your whole body in this place. Settle into a protected corner where you can watch, remember, feel, and reflect. Recall things you've experienced—sun, water, motion, movement—the heat of the sun, the texture of the water, the movement of light past your eyes, and the motion of things around you.

Build out and around from this place in which you've placed

Hypnagogic Lucidity

yourself. Imagine zooming in to magnify by ten what's right in front of you. Maybe, it's a table. Maybe, it's the ground at your feet. Maybe, it's the back of your hand. And zoom in again to the level of what's invisible, and you won't see it, so you imagine it. The cable-threads of the table cloth, the mountainous grains of dirt and dust, the creases and crevices of your magnified skin textured like a glacier.

And zooming out a power of ten, and then zoom out again to see all that's around you, outside your room or building, field or glade. Out into the landscape of forest, shore, or neighborhood. If it's a building, how tall is it? If it's a landscape, how wide is it? If it's a disembodied field, some unfamiliar place, then what might exist beyond the shadows and lights. Build a framework of some kind in the empty field you have not filled.

What energies flow through this, outside the story of your imagination? Is there an architect of your dreams? Who builds the sets, writes the scripts, and sews the costumes? Is there an author or just a continuous flow of action which, like a river, you dip into and out comes a childhood memory, yesterday's conundrum, or a willful plan?

Remember who you are in these times, when you're not your normal self. No one is watching you, and anyone is watching you. You are everything and anything, or you can be nothing at all. Hold on even then and consider what you have grasp of. Is there really a "you," or are you just memories and reactions? If you had the free will to manifest anything, what would you choose? What might you be if but for a moment... and what about the next moment?

Becoming Lucid

You are a shape-shifter. There is the shape you've always been, and the shape you've never been. How might you feel to take such a shape as you've never been before? Consider it's only temporary, as a bird, a fish, an old man, or a baby.

Do you remember your childhood? Can you imagine what it felt like when you were in that skin? Did it feel anything like today? Think of how quickly you could jump, how you fought against going to sleep and the long torpor of dragging yourself awake. Did your clothes fit you? The wound-up endless circles you could turn, and how you could run so fast you felt your legs would fall off. It's not like that anymore. Same self but different sensations. We hardly remember, yet we always recreate ourselves from memories. Just as we create others and how they feel and act from our imaginations.

Imagine a red sun, set in a yellow sky, beneath a purple twilight. Slow it all down, as dusk birds make their nests, and fish settle down to sleep. The red sun has a penetrating heat.

Relax now. Take a breath… and slowly let it out. Shrink the sun to a red dot moving around you like a second hand, caressing your temples, cheeks, ears, and the nape of your neck. Feel it circle around your neck, down to the dimple at the center of your collar bone.

Let this ball of light spiral around and down your body, slowly circling your ribs, your waist, the top of your pelvis, your hips. First down one leg, past your knee, shin, ankle, around the ball of your foot to your toes. Then at the top of the other hip and down the other leg, knee, shin, ankle, ball of your foot to your toes.

Feel this energetic ball make slow circles around you, cutting a path of spirals, receiving energy as if you are an antenna. Be alert for odd sounds and sensations, as you settle into your most central emotions, the feelings you have for yourself when all your thoughts are gone. Grasp the texture of this feeling, whether it's thick or thin, stout or fragile, inflamed or flaccid.

Imagine your inner-self as a larger beast, something you ride upon, that bears you forward. You are in the saddle, and you grasp the reins with poise and balance. Feel clear and centered. Calm, focused and well-supported. You are mounted upon an ally that knows your thoughts and is directed by your feelings. Ride this inward feeling forward through the veil into other realms. One… two… three… you're there. On you go, riding over the horizon, and we're done.

7 Dreaming Lucidity

"It is the ability to separate oneself from the current reality, and in some sense observe it, that seems to be a common element that leads to the insight that one is dreaming."

— Patrick Bourke, Hannah Shaw, (2014). "Spontaneous Lucid Dreaming Frequency and Waking Insight", in *Dreaming*, Vol. 24 (2).

Existing as part of the whole, animals are aligned with the whole. By thinking and acting from will, humans exist, in this analysis, out of connection and natural context.

Dreaming lucidity is a conundrum we must understand. Dreaming and lucidity are states of consciousness you can mix like red and blue to make shades of purple. Observing a lucid dream is like watching a movie, and when you watch a movie you cannot distinguish the scripted parts from those that are improvised. It's not the content of a dream that determines whether or not the dream is lucid—after all, you are the dream—it's whether you can guide the dream with your intentions.

This is too much to ask of ourselves. Under unusual situations, some people have acted in their dreams according to plans they made while they were awake. Even this does not prove lucidity, as your wakeful intentions could be part of your dream's script. Dreaming lucidity is actually the same as the question of free will. Whether or not we have waking free will has never been determined, and it is not our goal to resolve that question during sleep. Here, we are satisfied with shades of purple—shades of feeling lucid.

In a dream I had last night, I resolved to use the power of my dream to evoke the gremlin spirits. I attempted to do this by laying slices of cucumber in a grid pattern in the cupboard. I laid out the cucumber slices, but the gremlins didn't appear. I wasn't making much sense, but I was lucid.

Our goal is simply to think we are lucid while dreaming, to believe we have the free will to reflect and decide. This free will is no more real than free will in our waking life, for which there is no clear definition. Let it suffice for us to think we are lucid. This is an accomplishment.

The feeling we're looking to have in a dream is the feeling of self-knowledge, and this differs from simply riding the flow, accepting without question whatever appears. We're looking to feel that we're writing our own script, picking it out of the air on our own accord, improvising. We are not worrying too much about what person decided, or what forces came together, to write it.

Here, then, is your clarity: to dream in such a state as will allow you to say, "I am." And from that point you will say, "I want…" and "I will do…". In that, the giant decides to pick the fruit, or to fly, or whatever you are or want to do. And because "you are," you are able to reflect on what you've done, and say, "I'm flying!"

It is a next step to say, "I'm dreaming," but not such a big step.

Dreaming or flying; what's the difference? The difference is one of choice and consequences. To say, "I'm flying," means you've chosen an action. To say, "I'm dreaming," means you've chosen a different state of being, another step toward self-awareness.

You have two steps to take. The first is to decide, seemingly of your own will, to take an action. The second, also of your own will, is to conceive of a different reality. But, you'll notice, to say that you're dreaming doesn't make clear what else you could be. You could say that to yourself right now, and it is true that you are, but it's not illuminating.

There is a third step beyond recognizing that you're dreaming and that is to recognize what exists beyond your dream. You could take that step now, in your waking state, as well. This third step is the big step, and it takes us outside our known consciousness and outside this narrative. It is well worth considering, and it's something you should ask for. When in your dream, stop everything and exhort, "This is an illusion. Show me what is real!" I cannot tell you what will happen.

Dreaming Practice

Lucidity is disruptive. The charge of self-aware energy can easily tear through the fabric of the dream space and wake you up. You want to remain in the dreaming state of mind, becoming sort of awake, but not waking up. This is a paradoxical state. In a fully awake state, you would reject or be frightened by anything that was unreal, but here you want to accept, even encourage, the unreal.

Don't be too rational. If you're in a dream, and you need a car, do not go looking for your car. Do not go searching for a car rental office. Simply manifest a car. To pursue the rational in the dream world has been, for me, a recipe for failure. You're asking for a mixture of discernment and irrationality that is not part of a normal dream.

Exercises

— **Dream Exercise #1**: Lucidity is not a state of action, it's a state of intention. Moving with lucidity in a dream is like walking on tissue paper; you cannot change direction quickly or it will tear. Recognize that the rest of the dream exists in a non-lucid state. Don't disrupt that part of your mind that is dreaming. Direct your action by shifting your focus and collecting your intention. Let changes manifest from your intentions, not your actions.

— **Dream Exercise #2**: The part of your mind that is lucid runs at a higher frequency than the part of your mind that is not. These higher frequencies give you the ability to reflect and respond. Tap into the emotional content of the landscape you find yourself in, and ask yourself how you might manifest these emotions more strongly.

— **Dream Exercise #3**: Consider yourself in service to the dream and the characters in it. Your purpose in the dream is to bring light, to enlighten. Move into a mindset of grace and service, recognizing that your lucidity gives you strength like lucidity in waking life. Ask the dream characters what they need, and how you can help them. If there are no characters to ask, ask the dream, which is a way of asking yourself.

— **Dream Exercise #4**: Gently test yourself frequently, as your tendency will be to slip into nonlucid dreaming. This will feel like the hypnagogic urge to sleep. Remain mentally active by talking or thinking to yourself, remaining aware of your dream body, examining or engaging it. Move through the dream in ways that won't wake up the dreaming mind. Try running, jumping, hovering, flying, or spinning. Recognize that you are only in control of a portion of your experience. If you lose control, you'll lose all control.

— **Dream Exercise #5**: If you find yourself losing your awareness or your dreamscape is breaking up, focus on your self-awareness. Focus on the movement of walking, spinning, singing, looking at your hands, flying, or some other emotionally stable, self-aware activity. Relax any attempt to hold or fix the dream environment, let it change. Hold to self-awareness.

— **Dream Exercise #6**: If the dream becomes uncomfortable or an important idea arises, then wake yourself up by raising your voice or acting to interfere with the dream. Take control through direct involvement, at an intentional level, by sculpting something new in sound, or voice, or sight. Say to yourself, "I need to remember this," "This is over," or "I'm rising to another place."

— **Dream Exercise #7**: It is yet a higher level of lucidity to recognize your dream world is unreal, a *Truman Show* fiction. Such a realization may arise with frustration or confusion, with a knowledge that you are in a creation, or might be. Find the presence of mind to look toward and beyond your horizon. Call for explanation or transformation. Ask for the truth, and then hold on.

"Throwing yourself into it begins with being grateful that you even have something to throw yourself into."

— Rob Bell, from *How to Be Here: A Guide to Creating a Life Worth Living.*

Hypnotic Session 7

Stepping Off audio file at:
https://www.mindstrengthbalance.com/becoming-lucid-audio/

Stepping Off

Relax, step back, and take a slow breath. Feel it swell your chest like a snapshot of an inflated airbag. As it deflates and all air escapes from it you're left limp, hanging off your ribcage like the remnants of an explosion of microwaved spaghetti. Inhale... exhale... Just empty and relaxed inside your ribs.

Close the elevator doors of your eyelids. Let your eyelids lock down, so that to open your eyes is like forcing open the doors of your elevator. It won't go anywhere until you let go. Let those doors close, feel their weight, feel them safely closed, and don't touch them.

Let your elevator eyes descend down through your cheeks, down through your mouth, down through your neck, to drop into the subterranean cavern of your chest. A drop of water falling from a high ceiling... into a wide pool. Inhale... exhale... down into yourself.

Let go of your viewing tube, those blinders that block the range of what you see. You want to gaze around yourself with full lucidity, to see what's connected farther away, and allow what might not be connected at all. Be realistic: most of what you see, you see without seeing what it's connected to. Most actions you observe, you don't know what caused them.

Becoming Lucid

You see the trees move, you infer the wind. You see the world alight, you assume this is the sun. You watch people act, you expect a reason. You listen to yourself think, you believe intelligence. Forget these presumptions; they're just theories. You don't know what they mean, anyway. Let go of your viewing tube.

Dreams are thought-responsive; mindset is key. What you think is what you get; it's also what you fear. You don't have to dream to see this; we'll do it now.

Just let yourself slip farther down into yourself. Place your attention in your hands. Relax your hands, and feel your hands becoming warm and heavy. Feel the blood in your hands gradually funneling down, through your wrists, making your hands expand, widen, deepen. Feel the pulse in your hands. It may seem weak at first, but notice it's not a beat but a swell like a wave hitting a breakwater.

Sit with this pulse for a while. Follow your pulse down to a point where you're not thinking about what you're thinking about; you're just letting thoughts blow past like moisture in moving fog. It will wet your clothes, if you stand in it, so don't. Just stand aside, out of the wind, and see the thoughts go past.

What is your most likely thought? What is your most present inclination? Intention outwardly expressed, what person are you thinking of? It's a thought grazing in the field of your subconsciousness mind. Recognize, corral, and harness your inclination. It is someone, and focus on this person. They know you're looking at them. Don't deny your attention; engage it. They are familiar. They are resident in your mind.

Dreaming Lucidity

They are changing now. They are getting older, or wiser. They're evolving. You can see this is so if you don't look right at them. Look askance, just off to one side, and think of them as they change, and what they are changing from, and what they're changing into.

Notice all things: color, shape, form, and texture. Are they becoming more or less clear? Are they becoming more or less present? Are they becoming more or less part of your world? Bring the image of them closer, closer... close enough to see the hairs on their skin, and the fine wrinkles. Now slide them away, back to where they were, back beyond that into the background, then into the distance, now onto a cloud, now floating on a cloud, moving through the sky, to circle the horizon, always somewhere in the distance, never too far. Let them watch you from afar, in their position on this cloud.

Get a sense of yourself. Sense your point of view and of where this view comes from. Shift your focus to yourself, and notice if you are yourself solid or absent; moving, fixed, or fluid. Think of yourself as fluid, flexible, smooth, and stretchable. Feel that flexibility in your spine, your shoulders, your neck. Feel that fluidity in your lungs as you breathe and in your upper arms, motionless, held to you by rubber bands, rotating on gimbals and ball bearings.

Try a simple experiment: imagine spinning in a circle, just spinning in place, shifting your feet in simple dance steps, or pirouetting on a turntable. Slowly spinning in a circle, head held still on your neck, not getting dizzy, just watching the world pass like a distant horizon out a train's window. And out the window, the horizon circles beyond distant fields and around, beyond distant hills and around, and there are mountains in the distance. And as you keep turning there appears a shore and then a lake stretching into a valley.

Now say, "I am that lake," and be that lake, resting in a valley with untouched rocky shores. And you've settled down, and you've stopped turning. You're looking out over the water with its silky feeling across your hands and feet. And what would a lake feel like cupped in the gentle bowl of the valley?

Held up by dust-filled mud, held back by valley walls, leaking slowly through porous rock, rippling softly through a silver ribbon at the valley's open end. Consummately level across your surface, intimately responsive to the wind, acutely aware of all the earth's vibrations. A body of water, yes, but alive with vibration, fed by the blood of the mountain snows with beaches moist like lips beckoning aster, fireweed, bluebell, and buttercup shores. Flowers that turn brilliant heads toward a mountain sun, visited by moths, syrphids, dragonflies, and bumble bees.

And now say, "I am a bee," and be one. Encased in armor, bristling with fur, suspended from a vibrating aerial coatrack of wings, driven with intoxication from one explosion of colored flower petal to the next and there, inebriated with nectar, bumbling in every crease and crevice, titillated by the textures of fur against fur, barely sentient against the scent, completely addicted to your bee-ing, utterly at home in the warm sun, driving like a drunken bumper car to collide from one flower to the next. Your eyes psychedelic, a kaleidoscope of colors on a spectrum wider than human, to the drone of the music of your wings humming along the lake shore. A long lake shore, a long, egg shaped lake shore, a colored boundary around a circle of reflected clouds. Of whites, and blues, and deep black waters.

And now choose to be a cloud, to be shot from a flat and shimmering image to that three-dimensional being somewhere turning from invisible vapor to the foggy white of reflecting droplets. Traveling sightless, spaceless white, arcing eye of an arrow shot from a longbow, slipping relaxed and effortless, weightless to the peak of its arc, a state indiscernible to you in your weightless motion. Long body slowly rotating, fletch feathered, steepening angle entering your descent, exiting the cloud, spit out like a watermelon seed, open to the yawning earth below.

Choose to look back up toward the cloud, up toward the sky. And there is nothing but sky, as all the earth is below the horizon, and all that you can see is above it, everywhere, all around you. Falling backwards, feeling weightless, only mindful, residing somewhere, inside of something.

Spread your arms, and become a paper airplane tossed with a flick of the wrist, quick on your trajectory, bending in the air pressure of your paper wings to loop, and glide, and skim the surface. Twist and bank and be caught in the hand of yourself, as a child, as you once were.

Jump into that childhood, long since outgrown like a pair of socks, and remember a time when you ran so fast you almost fell over. What do you remember of who you were? And can you say to yourself, "I will remember who I was, when I was young." And they say we remember all we have experienced, stored somewhere in our memory, so remember this; the time when you were six, or eight, or ten.

Remember something that troubled you then and since this is a vision, you can fix it. Maybe you were disappointed, falsely accused, or unfairly punished. Simply take this memory and bend it. Memory is plastic, little of what we remember is factually true, and we can feel imagined visions with degrees of emotion that match the authentic.

If you felt unappreciated, dispose of that memory and recall those who did appreciate you. As if you were fixing a pothole, clean the detritus from the hole in your self-image, and fill that hole with the love of those who really knew you. There is no question that their love for you was deeper than the disrespect of others. Why remember and relive your collision with misfortune when, at the same time but different place, others loved you?

Repairing memory is akin to redirecting your emotion in a dream. To consciously take the bothersome and shrink its memory in all dimensions is like acting with lucidity in a dream to take a bothersome feeling and reshape it. In the dream, you ask the agonist, "What do you have to tell me; how can I ease your disquiet?" In waking life, you address your recollection and ask, "Of what are these feelings built; with what inner strengths can I resolve or avoid the suffering of others?"

Recall your child self, and picture yourself as you were, and as you felt. Speak to yourself, as a person who you once knew, and who still resides inside you in habits, pathways, loves, and actions.

Say to your child self, "I loved you. I did my best to protect myself. I am at no fault, and you carry no guilt. I will recall you, and I can fill those absences that were abandoned and never filled. I was wise, and you are wise, and we will honor each other."

Anchor your connection with an action. Recall something you really valued once, when you were young. Imagine this thing in detail, color, weight, and texture. Imagine it as you once held it in your hands, and then accept it as a gift your child-self gives to you. Recall the kinds of things that you really liked when you were young. I loved miniature diecast metal war tanks when I was 9, beautifully painted with tiny moving parts. Locate the closest thing you can find today, things you once cherished, and buy one for yourself, if you can afford it. At least take yourself to see. Just for yourself.

This is not a lucid dream, but you have changed the way you feel, and you have created this for yourself. Your memory is not history, it is alive and active. Your memory can speak, and that is what occurs in your dreams. If you are quiet and open, you can be in that state now. And if you can be there now, you can return here in your dreams. Practice here what happens there. There is a reflection between dreams and imagination. Manage your emotions here, and your strength will carry into dreaming.

Leave this now and return. The elevator of awareness stands on the lakeshore, glass cube suspended from a cable, your own version of Doctor Who's time- and space-warping police box. The door opens; you step inside; it closes and the elevator begins to hum.

Becoming Lucid

Counting down:

10, as you begin to ascend, the landscape falls below you.

9, above the ridgeline and things appear distant far below.

8, the sky darkens to asur as clouds sweep past from above.

7, the horizon grows hazy, the air colder and the azure sky a darker blue.

6, clouds fog past, the ground a smear of color, a scimitar's curving edge.

5, the horizon's circle falls below, the earth drifts away, hove to an ocean of sky.

4, black all around, the sun sucks in the skylight, stars appear dense and steady.

3, floating, motionless, weightless—aware only of your body and the cube around you.

2, you are the only presence, aware, watching, calm, peaceful, and alert.

1, ready to open your eyes to see yourself floating in this dream. Encased in the elevator that is your body, parked in this room, moving through space.

And you're back.

Dreaming Lucidity

8 Hypnopompic Lucidity

"Waking up begins with saying am and now. That which has awoken then lies for a while staring up at the ceiling and down into itself until it has recognized I, and therefrom deduced I am, I am now."
—Christopher Isherwood, from *A Single Man*.

Waking up from a dream feels similar to waking up in the shower. It's startling, and you don't know how you got there. There are cases where I've woken myself up, and it has been a relief. In those cases, I do know how I got here: I brought myself here.

This begs the question of where "here" is. If here is a place that one makes for oneself, then just how real is it? "Oh," we might tell ourselves—if we had to think about it—"This is the real here, and before was a 'here' of my imagination." True as that might be, it's a pretty tepid lie.

The hypnopompic state is your last chance to stew in your emotions before reason returns. It's not your only chance—you can be wholly emotional at other times—but it's usually your last chance before rationally organized reality reimposes itself. It's like saying goodbye to your loved ones: you'd like to make it last, but you know it won't. But here, if you have the time, it might.

There are two things you can do from the hypnopompic state; you have two choices. You can wake up, or you can go back to sleep. Actually you have four choices: you can take either of those two actions with intention or without. That's really the topic of this chapter: how to make the two intentional choices.

To wake up intentionally is to take stock of all your feelings, before they slip away. This means getting in touch both with how your body feels, and with what's on your mind. That may mean recalling your night's dream-narrative or simply sitting with the last and most present emotions you have. You choose which side of the bed you're going to get out of. You have many choices because until you've decided what your shape is, all sorts of daytime attitudes will suit you.

If you're feeling wronged then, by all means, get out of the wronged side of the bed. If you feel entirely well-assembled, then you might choose to hit the ground running. If you're like me—and I don't know how many people are like me—then you won't exactly know how you feel. I think that's accurate, because knowing and feeling are incompatible complements. Feeling is broad and diffuse, while knowing is clear and precise. In hypnagogia, you have the blessed confluence of both and however that washes out, we should relish this.

Dreams conflate the reasonable and the unreasonable. They combine elements that are definite with elements that are vague and ineffable. This is essential to what we call dreaming. Recognize and amplify this. As you reflect on the dream amplify the differences between your thoughts and your feelings, between elements that are definite in time and space, and influences that are indefinite. The message of the dream lies in this mixture. Watch for these boundaries.

This remains true, should you decide to return to sleep. Perhaps it's even more important to embrace this duality when you return to sleep, because dreams embody duality: characters of reason acting on a landscape of emotion. Before returning to sleep, resolve which characters, places, and actions to encourage or discourage.

Get in touch with the "reasons" that underlie these feelings which—because they are feelings—are not reasons at all. Let yourself, your characters, and their situations sink into an ocean of feelings. A boundless, shoreless, bottomless sense of roiling emotion encroaching like nightfall, as you fall back to sleep. That's what it means to return to sleep with intention.

Hypnopompic Practice

The waking up space is similar to the falling asleep space, but you're moving in the other direction. You are again dissociated and witness to floating images, feelings, and ideas, but you're moving toward greater alertness. In the hypnopompic state, you want to slow down, remain settled, and relinquish the urge to greater clarity. Retain the subtle fabric: whispered ideas and flowing energy. If your will is lucid dreaming, then aim to re-submerge, return or re-envelope yourself in your dreamscape, and enter a new dream.

Exercises

— **Hypnopompic Exercise #1**: Attune to your body. Focus on the sensations. If you are comfortable, then do not move. If you could be more comfortable, then adjust yourself with as little movement as possible. Defer any consideration of waking events or the day ahead. Focus only on your nighttime thoughts and recollections.

Hypnopompic Lucidity

—**Hypnopompic Exercise #2**: If you want to re-enter your dreams, then explore Clare Johnson's stages of hypnagogia. If you want to exit your dreams, follow them in reverse.

1 - Clouds or waves of light or color: feeling relaxed and letting your thinking become still.

2 - Initial lights: recalling stars, sparks, or dots approaching, receding, or traversing your view.

3 - Static images: recalled from dreams as shapes, faces, and unrecognizable complexities.

4 - Transient three-dimensional images: replay short animated dream sequences.

5 - 3D scenes embedded in a narrative, carrying messages, motions, feelings, and associations.

— **Hypnopompic Exercise #3**: Review your last memories. Step through the dream and as new dream threads appear, assign each a placemark, as a means of returning to them. One might be assigned the name, "the beach," another, "the wall," a third, "my old school." You're trying to pull together a shape made out of smoke. Focus on your feelings. Let your feelings draw out the details.

— **Hypnopompic Exercise #4**: Relax and engage. For those images that create tension or distress, place yourself above, away, or at a distance from them. Build with your mind a stage set around the vision that sets it off, and make it a clear construction, one which you control, and which you can engage or disengage. If a dream element causes you discomfort, then consciously engage it for the purpose of revising it. If you recognize something that displeases you, correct it, defuse or de-energize it. If you're displeased with darkness, then bring in light. If you're displeased with an obstacle, then break it, remove it, or plant flowers in it. To make a strong element weaker, convert it from color to black and white. To make a dream element stronger enhance its colors, amplify its sounds, create anticipation in your body and make contact with it.

— **Hypnopompic Exercise #5**: Return to the modified dream. Once you have remembered the dream, reconnected with your feelings, and reengaged your thinking of it, then decide what you dislike and how it could be improved, what engages your curiosity and how it could be explored. What attracts you, and what would you like to indulge in more completely? Using your imagination, create what you want first as an idea, then as an image, and finally as an experience happening to you. As you do this, let your sense of time and place focus fully on the experience you're creating. Like catching a wave on a surfboard, let this experience take you. Stay relaxed, stay comfortable, stay in a reflective state of mind.

Hypnopompic Lucidity

"I know how much a dream can be worth, but, alas... 'Hello.'"
— Richard Brautigan, from his short story "The Library."

Hypnotic Session 8

Crossroads audio file at:
https://www.mindstrengthbalance.com/becoming-lucid-audio/

This session is intended to be listened to upon first waking up while still in a liminal hypnopompic state.

Crossroads

Bring yourself back to last night before you went to sleep. Recall what you did last night, and how you put your day away, embraced relaxation and maybe fatigue, and decided to get into bed. Recall, if you can, how you felt and what you might have thought before you went to sleep, and then imagine witnessing yourself falling asleep and beginning to dream.

Imagine you're lying on the vital earth. Imagine you're lying on a bed of moss. Imagine you're lying on the moss and earth-covered top of a large flat rock. Imagine you are lying on a bed of moss, set back from the edge of a small cliff, dropping in a series of rock steps, down into a forest-filled valley of sleep and shadows. Keep your eyes closed, your vision still, and your body motionless. Just float, as you are, in the border-world between earth and sky.

Above you is the indigo sky of a rising dawn and beyond is endless space. A space that really ends so far away that, if it ends at all, it extends beyond imagination. Here is where you have awoken, here is where you are: at the interface.

Where have you been? What have you seen? What can you

recall? A simple scene or a kaleidoscope of a story. Give each scene a word like the label on a slip below the body of a beetle pinned to your collection board. Give each scene a word, a dream collection of words, a collection of colored beetles, whose theme is situation, and whose situation tells the story. And if there is only one scene, then note the objects, elements, or feelings in it. Or maybe there is only one object that you can give several aspects like color, shape, or feeling.

I'll ask for four, even if you only see one or maybe none. Use your memory or imagination, imagine you thought a dream, and maybe you did. Let it open not as a book but as a collection. And if you remember only one, then put yourself in it, and imagine another... and another... and another, until you have four.

But less is OK too; it's enough to start with one. Consider it from four different angles. Or just one thing from one angle, if that's what you're comfortable to focus on. Whatever your heart presents to you. I'll count four, and you show these things to me, holding them up like cards in a game. One... two... three... four.

If you your dream is too thin, pick another, an old memory. Maybe a place you remember and from that place a scene. And if you have four scenes, recount those for me once again. One... What is the first scene? What are the colors in it? Two... What is the second scene? What's in the foreground, and what's in the distance? Three... The third. Call it to you, let it describe itself in name, shape, or sound. Was there motion? What was moving? And four, the last. Hold that scene, and look, examine. What exists at the edges, its boundary, or the end of the action?

Now bring up the feelings. Each has one, maybe they are all alike, maybe each a different flavor. What are the flavors of your dreams, of your memories? Imagine there is a connection between sight, smell, and taste. An image, a scent, a flavor.

I know this is a lot to ask, and you don't need to answer. Just consider the question. Turn each scene over in your mind, considering the details each might hold. And of course you make them up. That's what memory does for you—it's the store of your imagination.

One... What was that first scene? What did it feel like? What reaction did you feel in your body?

Two... The second scene. Imagine turning the illustrations of an old book. With each recognition comes a recollection and with that, a feeling.

Three... What message lies in your gut or comes from your heart? Warm, hard, comfortable, distant, or reassuring?

And the fourth—and remembering four things is asking quite a lot—so if there is not a fourth, let the fourth be a rest stop, an unlit stage, an empty diorama. But if there is content, even faint, how does it make you feel?

This is a catalog of a dream, real or one you've manufactured. How might it be different? What is calling to you? If these were events you had to live, or live again, what would you change? What would you like? And if you can imagine changing something—the scene, the dialog, or setting—would that make you sad or happy? These memories have messages, not each alone—separate as they might be—but all together.

Hypnopompic Lucidity

What if you could change your life? What if you could rewrite the script? What if you could change your feelings and reactions so that you saw things differently? Would you still make changes? Are the memories worth changing? Perhaps there are mistakes or misunderstandings. Perhaps they are the ravings of people upset, or exclamations of the illuminated and the joyful.

How does all this apply to you—to the things you did yesterday, or will do today? What if in these feelings exists a kind of guidance that can direct you toward changes in memory, habit, and desire?

Maybe time does not move simply forward but bleeds back a little from the day to come, like the wave in front of a boat, that rides in front of the hull that creates it. Do you create a swell in the future day that you haven't yet gotten to?

Maybe your fractured dream-tales are whispers of the future —warning you to be on guard, to be prepared—hinting as to how you might stay on-center. It's true that your mood will affect what you notice and how you react, and what you notice and how you react will affect your mood. And what you notice and your mood will affect your memory, and this will reflect back in contemplation.

There are things in the day to come that you do know about, your intuition may be more accurate than your use of intellect. Foreknowledge of the day ahead is not so mysterious, if you accept intuition as your guide. So the future may be buried in your dream-stories, and your moonshine-washed moods may be your future's truth.

Becoming Lucid

Time is not so one way and only one way, it's like waves in a small bathtub, reflecting back and forth, adding and subtracting. Let these ideas and images wash over you, passing through rapids too quick for details. Hold to the center of your emotion and let these other scenes parade along a stable balance beam.

As you exit from your hypnopompic state, drop your reasoning rudder and hoist your sails. The dream bits drain like fish thrown on the deck—a few of the big ones are stored and salted in the hold. Some people may hold their lucidity through seas of dreaming, but you won't be sailing your dream into the daytime. Stow your cargo, trim your mind-sails, and feel your boat listing under reality's pressure with the ballast of your emotion as your keel.

Now head into the wind of wakefulness with hair combed and face on straight. Tacking upwind, as it were, to don your day-sailing gear: bathed, dressed, focused, and wearing street shoes. Replace emotion with reason, dreams with reality, expression with obligation. Fold your wings.

But perhaps not so fast. Perhaps you can hold in your subtle heart the hearing and the wisdom of your night. Bring this with you with intention and appreciation. You know just what's to come and you will be part of it, and you know which part is you, and you will preserve that. Tied to the mast, as it were, to hear siren songs of reason but not to dash yourself on their rocks or leap into the beckoning sea.

And as I count up to ten, clear your head for thinking much like spreading drop clothes before painting. With reason and presence you'll catch the drips that fall from the roller brush of today's reality. One… two… three. Throwing down the drop cloths and gathering your gear. Four… five… six. Assembling your energy into your face, your eyes, your hands and feet. Seven… eight… nine. Feeling clear, composed, focused, and comfortable. And ten, ready to stand and open your eyes.

9 Beyond Lucidity

"We are in a jungle and find our way by trial and error, building our road behind us as we proceed."
— Max Born, from *Experiment and Theory in Physics*.

Perception

Time is our obstacle; we must find another kind of time. Living in the moment offers the most accurate experience of all things present, but we cannot hold much in the moment. For that reason, we expand the present with memories of the past and expectations of the future. This provides a longer duration and a larger place in which to organize. But our memories and expectations are inaccurate. Even when expanded, our memories and expectations are too small, too simple, and too linear to contain all the relationships we're made of and involved with.

To understand ourselves more deeply, we need to expand our limited sense of the present, our short memories, and our simple expectations. We can build a greater sense of self by developing our mind's connection to our body. We can achieve a shift in consciousness by understanding that our body stores awareness.

Your body experiences everything that affects you. Your mind experiences only what your body makes available to you. The mind analyzes signals. It does not perceive. It is your body that perceives and decides what signals to send to you.

If your eyes are frozen in a stare, your mind fixates on what it's experiencing, and your powers of reflection are weakened. In this way, situations that hijack your eyes entrain your mind. We like to tell ourselves this is our own decision, but often it is not: frightful, dangerous, satiating, pleasurable, sexual, and powerful images entrance us, regardless of our intention.

In those species we've examined, we've found this hijacking of awareness happens in the retina, not in the brain. The frog's retina filters its awareness. It's an evolutionary advantage to allow instinct to take over in imperative situations. If you hold to a separation of mind and body, then you must accept that the body, separate from your mind, is responsible for a good deal of what you take to be reality.

I do not subscribe to the separation of mind and body; I do not consider them separate. I can retreat inside my head and, in doing so, perceive them as separate, but that is a state of being. This apparent separation is newly evolved as a consequence of our prefrontal cortex; it is not fundamental. Through a greater connection to structures in my body and becoming more conversant with the messages of my body, I develop a larger and more nuanced past, present, and future.

Memory

We learn through interaction with and the rearrangement of the contents of our minds. Through reflection, discussion, inspiration, and confusion we construct new ideas. At this, our species is particularly adept. You might say that we are so creative because we are so fault-tolerant, so prone to error, and so persistent. We are self-creators far beyond any other species we know.

We learn through movement, and engaging people in our environment. This knowledge is not entirely abstracted into memories, patterns, and cellular structures, it is at least partly stored in our environmental creations, our social context, and our bodies. Aspects of our self-image are stored in our posture: our confidence, sexuality, courage, integrity, strength, health, alertness, excitement, and so forth—with these are associated concepts, memories, and processes. To omit our bodies, possessions, and created environment as repositories of identity is absurd.

We enshrine our identity in—and to varying extents limit our identity to—the physical and social structures we inhabit. For many of us, our identity depends on these attachments. When the pyramids were built, species-identity rested on the life-span of the structures created. Today, species-identity resides in the persistent themes of ephemeral communication.

It is an unsupported assumption that all memory resides in the brain. It is an unsupported assumption that memory exists in one particular form at all. The most we can do is correlate certain gross brain activities with gross aspects of some memories but such a sterile notion of memory—devoid of its triggers, context, and connections—is not recognizable as memory at all. It is certainly not what we experience with even the simplest of memories. Our current knowledge of the brain no more explains the mind, than archaeology explains life.

"... not all memories require sleep, but the more complex and elaborate the information to be learned, the more likely sleep will be

required for consolidation."
– Sara Mednick, Sean Drummond (2004). "Sleep: A Prescription For Insight?" *INSOM*, Vol. 3 (26).

States

There is "the state," and there is "the work." Your state is what fits within or is shaped by your awareness. "The work" is what you do from within a state.

States of mind are connections to awareness, and that awareness can be large or small, more or less, inclusive or exclusive. The "state" is the result of how you focus your awareness. Awareness is the noun, focus is the verb.

States differ, some more than others. One may say some classes of states are so different as to be disjointed, which is to say, unreachable from other states through a quantitative change: joy to sorrow, comfort to fear, respect to disdain. Other states differ in increments: agitation to anxiety, curiosity to attraction to obsession, appreciation to respect to reverence to abdication.

These paths meander from positive to negative, split into branches that allow us to make choices, though some choices may be short lived. These paths define an emotional surface with hills and valleys. It is the surface of our emotional body, and no two person's surfaces are the same.

Every point on this emotional surface is a state of mind. In some cases, we can slide from state to state. In other cases, we can only leap over or around, and sometimes we fall back. And still other states are not available to us now, in this moment, until further notice, or ever.

States support different structures which means different

concepts, constructions, realizations, and realities. Each person and what they have manifested for him or herself is an example of what has been realized from their state.

There is no one spectrum of states of mind common to all people. There seems to prevail some common notion of states that are larger or smaller, more or less balanced, more or less inclusive, more or less fertile. At one level, one can establish a state corresponding with every emotion, and there is no single emotional map common to everyone.

The Diagnostic and Statistical Manual (DSM)—created by the American Psychological Association and periodically updated—is a compendium of aberrant behavioral presentations. The DSM suggests these behaviors are the result of states of mind and that the origin of the imbalance lies in the individual. Most people—psychologists, therapists, and doctors included—do not understand this is only a suggestion. The DSM takes the mind-body split one step further and asserts that each mind-body—that is, each person—is separate, and each person's "flaws" are their own. This empowers those who meet the definition of normal and disempowers those who don't.

Clinical psychology in general—the DSM in particular—tells us little about ourselves as individuals. Clinical psychology has nothing to say about our sense of purpose, which is our work, and the realm of our dreams.

This is not absolutely true, as the field of transpersonal psychology tries to bridge this gap, but it is true for the most part, until further notice. Psychology is a collective state of mind, one that affects us as individuals. Every group that has its own attitude supports a collective state of mind. These collective states—states of group thinking—exist on yet another surface of collective emotions.

These surfaces are unexplored territories with their own evolutions and works to be done.

Works

The work is a noun; it is what you accomplish. Your work is emergent, that is to say, it is created from the materials of which you are aware; it is subjective. The work is not fundamental in the sense that your work does not pre-exist the person you are. The work is not objective. It is not separate from who you or we are. We must interact with our creations for them to have any meaning.

There is a reflexive principle here: from our state emerges our work, yet our work is the scaffolding of our state. At its most fundamental, our work is what we identify with and remember. It feels separate from us. Without identification and memory, our work is lost, and we are lost. In a fully subjective sense, what we create results from the state we're in, and our creations define us. We are our work.

Lucidity

Lucidity is the ability to consciously act from some point within your personal range of states. The key word is "consciously," a relative term. From this point, going beyond lucidity means expanding your awareness, your depth of focus, the scope of your interaction, and the range of your creation. Lucid dreaming is an effort to breach one of these thresholds. The ubiquity of this threshold—sleep—and the difficulty in crossing it—to enact free will in dreams—makes this project interesting. There are myriad other states and myriad other crossings. You can become lucid in your profession, your religion, or your emotional state.

It seems we can equate different people's dream states because, while the content is different, the dream state is largely devoid of personality. Our personality appears in what populates our dreams; our personality resides in the symbols. When fully inflated, the dream presents the ego and, as long as we remain non-lucid, we are actors and audiences but not directors. Because we have scant measure by which to compare one waking state to another—which is to say one lucid state to another—we cannot make accurate comparisons between different people's state of dream lucidity. No two free-wills are the same.

It has been reported, and it stands to reason, that the depth and import of your lucid dream experience can be enhanced by contemplating yourself into a deep and meaningful state of mind before going to sleep. This is consistent with all that we've said thus far, but the point deserves repeating: be in your most empowered waking state before sleep, in order to most empower your dream experience. Inhabit your freest of wills before going to sleep.

Theory of Dreams

We cannot understand lucidity until we understand dreams. If we do not understand what it is to be in a dream, then we cannot understand the process of stepping out of one. We need a dream theory, so here is one.

Dreams are a self-exploration of our emotional world. Our emotional world is all of what we believe in. It consists of all our feelings, and the relationships and dynamics between our feelings. That is to say, how we are caught up in feelings. Our emotional world is our emotional landscape and movement through our emotional landscape.

We participate in normal dream experience, as participation is what generates emotion. Full participation is the mechanism of emotion. The dream happens to us, we are not separate from it, and it is fully believable. "Lucidity" means being separate from the dream, or from its direct experience. To be lucid means to reflect upon something as separate from us. The benefit of lucidity is perspective; the drawback of lucidity is a lack of detail in the immediacy of the experience.

Utility

What's gained or lost in being lucid depends on the emotional territory you're experiencing, and whether the additional awareness you gain through separation results in greater or less understanding. I use the word "understanding" to represent any form of growth which includes integration, inspiration, resolution, relief, empowerment, or transformation. Gaining perspective may allow you to see alternatives; losing immediacy may prevent you from seeing the situation's silver lining.

Consider one example of where lucidity may help you and another example of where it may not. The first example is sadness, and this could be the sadness of loss, separation, or heartbreak. In a dream of sadness, you may be trapped in a landscape of grief without hope of resolution. This is your emotional landscape, and it has been designed, or assembled, in such a way that there is no way out.

In this dream, becoming lucid allows you to recognize your predicament and to ask for the liberation of which you can conceive but not experience. It is often said that you should not confront or contradict dream characters, as this is to deny them as a symbol. To reject a dream element is to deny a part of yourself, something that your intellect does not have the power to do. What your intellect can do, however, is to become open to greater experience and to a more resolving experience whether this be pleasant or not.

Becoming Lucid

In a dream of grief, becoming lucid enables you to soften hard boundaries and explore the sharp, scorching, unscalable walls of your container. This is a call for guidance out of the torment in which you're stuck. Lucidity is not guidance itself but a call for it. Lucidity does not control your emotions but allows an exit from the paralysis of your configuration.

The second example is wonder. There are frontiers in our emotional landscape beyond which we are overwhelmed and where we don't know what to feel. It's not clear what we're overwhelmed with, as the emotion can be so strong as to be unfamiliar. We don't know how to react.

If you find yourself in this position, any choice will come from ignorance. Any form, action, or interpretation that you project will reflect your own limitations. The only enabling conscious choice you can make is to be open, which is not to make any conscious choice at all. This is the choice to be vulnerable, and it requires a good measure of strength.

The more empowering choice, in a landscape of wonder, is to avoid navigating back to the world of the familiar. The empowering lucid choice is just to let go and be swept into the dream more deeply. There, if you can remember the dream, you may find inspiration.

> *"At the words 'letting go,' I realize that I'm dreaming, and that the real solution is to trust and let go. As I do so, leaping into the beautiful sunrise sky, I am overwhelmed with feeling, and awaken with tears of joy."*
>
> —Steven LaBerge, from "Varieties of lucid dreaming experience," in R.G. Kunzendorf & B. Wallace (Eds.), *Individual Differences in Conscious Experience.*

I was once pulled off a mountainside and went spinning into the void. After a few revolutions, with no way to regain myself, I resolved to be as aware as possible and not to panic. As if doing some elaborate, spinning, high-dive maneuver I watched the world spin a few more 360-degree revolutions before coming to an abrupt stop in a shallow snowbowl. I was relaxed and unhurt; I had no emotional trauma to release. I had chosen to relax in the unfamiliar reality. Because it ended well, the memory is empowering. This was reality and I was really lucky, but had it been a dream it would have felt just as real.

Beyond Dreaming

In both of these examples—and regardless of how lucid you are in these sorts of dreams or choose to be—the work is not over when the dream ends. The purpose of these dreams, and the call to expend effort in the direction in which they lead, is to further the expansion of your self-awareness.

In order to accomplish this, it is essential to see that this is not dream work or sleep work; it's life work. If the dream provided the overture, your waking life must hear the symphony. And just as it is unclear where dreams come from, it's also unclear where ideas come from. It's not clear who wrote the overture, and it's not clear who writes the symphony. Your understanding grows just in the hearing of it.

To complete the exercise of dreams, then, involves not only adding elements of wakefulness to your dreams but adding what you dream of in your waking life. For some, this may mean living a dream. For others, it may mean living in a dream. The result will depend on how you conduct your affairs.

The exercise beyond dreaming is to see your dreams in waking life—to see the emotional landscape of your waking life as following the same contours as were revealed to you in your dreams. It is not the signs of the dreams that are real, but the topography of the landscape on which these signs appear. The dream tells not only of the meaning of its signs but of the contour of the landscape of your emotions. That is not a dream landscape; it's real.

Beyond Lucidity

Going beyond lucidity is understanding that being lucid is about being aware, not being in control. Awareness is organic; awareness grows. It may germinate in a dream, and lucidity may help shed the seed-coat, but the promise of awareness lies in what it can grow into. Nurturing a new awareness involves recognizing and attending to it, as nurturing any new life requires.

At the simplest level, you must continue to feel it and, in this regard, it's not necessary to remember the details. Your willful, analytical, intellectual, lucid memory is not required. What is required is to make a new place, for a new feeling, in the landscape of your emotions and to allow that feeling to grow.

I have avoided making value judgements. Judgements are relative to the facts of the matter, and I have no facts. In the following exercises, you will find negative as well as positive feelings. Both are equally valid, both are equally potent.

Consider the landscape of your emotions as hills and valleys. Life situations affect, afflict, assault, or assure you. Being a "whole person" means receiving, digesting, and orienting yourself to prevail in the face of these effects. This requires your ability to respond from anywhere in your emotional landscape. Your pathways cover the territory like a fine net, like a mycelial mat, connecting each point. You are resilient and able to restore yourself from any deformation.

Some of your emotional landscape involves suffering. There are pits, caves, cliffs, and peaks. Their exploration will yield elation, inspiration, affirmation but also pain and suffering. You had best be your own judge in navigating this terrain.

If you move alone, you can be independent. If you are enmeshed in partnership, family, or community you are not independent—at least it would be irresponsible to act with disregard for those you'll affect. You have your greatest freedom when you are of no immediate concern to others. And this is why, I believe, your greatest opportunity to explore your emotional landscape is in your dreams.

Judgements are relative to events and outcomes, and these are relative to the timespan in which they occur. Because these timespans can be long—especially with regard to long-repeated and deeply ingrained patterns—it pays to be patient and strong.

It also pays to be pain-tolerant. They say, "Pain is necessary, suffering is optional." They mean pain is a perception you cannot deny, while suffering is an emotion that you can reject. The truth is even perception can be denied, and here is the strength of lucidity: you can focus on or away from anything.

Before judging, arrange the evidence. Don't accept what you first perceive; you can rearrange perception. Lucidity is both rearranging the evidence and making the judgement. To go beyond lucidity is to recognize there are emotional areas in which you are not able to do either. To go beyond lucidity is to maintain awareness as you enter into states where you have never been before.

Exercises

Becoming familiar with the boundaries of your sense of self.

— **End Exercise #1**: At a time when there is no pressing

concern, no interruption, and nothing further to be done, sit by yourself and think about nothing as hard as you can. I don't mean not to think. I mean to think about things that are or amount to nothing. You can easily do this by filling your mind with disconnected and nonsensical words. After you have done this for a while, reflect on how similar this is to your normal stream of thoughts.

— **End Exercise #2**: At a time when there is no pressing concern, interruption, or anything further to be done, sit by yourself in a place where there is plentiful sound, preferably a variety of different sounds. Attach your attention to each passing sound and amplify it to the point of becoming annoying. Assign to each sound a texture, or a color, or a shape, or an emotion, and let these forms of synesthesia move from sound to sound. Done with sufficient gusto, this should soon become irritating. At that point, detach from your awareness, and allow yourself to float away from the sounds without any attachment. Turn your attention inward to a complete silence and try, if you can, not to hear anything at all.

— **End Exercise #3**: From a calm, empty, and relaxed position, such as previously described, feel the worst of possible outcomes for your life. I don't mean that you should think about it, as in the scenes, events, and outcomes, as that creates an engulfing immersion in depression. Rather than drowning yourself, feel as few details as necessary to evoke in yourself an utterly hopeless, vacant, and pointless sense of self. Avoid the facts; embrace the emotion.

Once you have created this dismal state—and you need not grasp or indulge yourself in it—step back from it. See it as your creation: a spot lit stage in an ink dark theatre. Then shut off all the lights so that all is black, and rich, and entirely formless. In that black, rich, formless dark there is absolutely nothing: nothing bad, nothing good, no air, no breath... just nothing. It's not a place you can reside, but it's a real place. Feel this place outside yourself, and let your dismal-self collapse into it. Feel yourself clear, free, and open.

— **End Exercise #4**: This inverse of the previous exercise should be done alternately with it. From a calm, empty, and relaxed position, feel the best of possible outcomes for your life. Don't think about it in too much detail, as that creates an overwhelmingly saccharine disequilibrium, a state of almost headstrong nausea. Avoid a manic excursion by limiting yourself to as few details as necessary to evoke utter exuberance. Avoid the facts; embrace the emotion which is, oddly enough, a rather drunk, vacant, and pointless sense of self.

Once you have created this euphoric state, step back from it. See it as your creation: a spot lit stage in an ink dark theatre. Then shut off all the lights, so that all is black and rich and entirely formless. In that black, rich, formless dark, there is absolutely nothing: nothing bad, nothing good, no air, no breath... just nothing. It's not a place you can reside, but it's a real place. Feel this place outside yourself, and let your euphoric-self collapse into it. Feel yourself clear, free, and open.

— **End Exercise #5**: If you've completed the previous two exercises, compare your negative world with your positive world. Consider the differences. Was one more emotional than the other? Was one stronger, more realistic or artificial than the other? If one seemed more "real," why? If the negative was more repellent than the positive was attractive, why? If you found yourself unable to believe in what you were creating or unwilling to flesh out all the feelings that were stirred up, then which ones presented difficulty and why?

Sit with those particular issues and have a chat. Bring your normal self, your negative, and your positive perspectives into a three-way discussion as equals. Can you all be allies, or will you be adversaries? Resolve to make room for and to create reconciliation between the negative vision and the positive dream.

"We don't have a strong grasp of what reality 'out there' even is, because we detect such an unbearably small slice of it."
— David Eagleman, neuroscientist, quoted in *The Guardian*, April 29, 2012.

Hypnotic Session 9

Welcome to The End audio file at:
https://www.mindstrengthbalance.com/becoming-lucid-audio/

Welcome to The End

Let's do an exercise of going beyond mind. It's a simple matter of putting yourself at the end of things and then going further. We'll create four situations like situations in lucid dreams where we face the author of our conceptions and ask, "What's really here?"

Settle down and settle in. Focus on your pulse and follow it as you inhale, wait a heartbeat, and then exhale. Focus on your breath. Watch it bellow in... and then bellow out.

Imagine a tall water wheel—turned slowly by the pressure of a sluiced and collared stream—each heartbeat pushing a paddle of the wheel. At a point on the wheel's edge, a creaky pushrod is attached and on each first half-turn, the rod advances. On each second half-turn, it retreats. Inflating and deflating... and your breath... inhales... and exhales.

Picture the stream that fills and turns this wheel. This wheel that blocks the stream, that flows from its reservoir, a reservoir that slowly fills and slowly drains. It fills slowly, rising at the rate of a turning second hand; a red line sweeping across a clock's face; a low fog passing on an offshore breeze.

Sink down deeper, two breaths down, twice as relaxed. Inhale... exhale... And inhale again... and exhale again. With this half-cycle the reservoir fills and with two more breaths—inhale... exhale... and again... inhale... exhale—the reservoir empties. Follow it, dropping down step by step, more relaxed, more released, more aware of the turning of the second hand... the moving of the fog. Breathe as slowly as the second hand... 5... 10... 15... slow... slower... slowest.

You feel like water: loose and formless; held in shape by your container, able to flow into any shape, to hold any idea, any picture. Feel your body as the surface of a stream, rippling, mumbling, orchestrating all of your rhythms so that everything pulses to your heart beat. Tic, toc... tic, toc. No concerns, nothing further to be done. Just listen to these sounds.

In this first situation, attend to each passing sound. Feel each sound as a texture, a color, a shape. Some are soft drones and others sharp cymbals. Create in your mind a picture of what is creating each sound. How many pictures you can remember, how many different sounds there are? When you listen to one sound, and you hear it again, maybe over and over again, how do the sounds change? Do they wobble in pitch? Do they alternate in intensity?

What do you hear when the sounds fade? Do you hear a hum, a drone, ringing, or silence? As the sounds grow, make the sounds bigger, amplifying them in your perception. As the sounds fade, make them fainter, then make the sounds smaller, then make the sounds move farther away.

Listen to each sound again. Imagine that what you're hearing is not what you think. What if it's not a car, or a plane? What else could it be? What if it's not a horn? What else could it be? Some sounds are just echoes lost in their origin and jumbled in reflection. Sounds distort, voices sound like sirens, traffic like waves, and water like curtains.

Musical instruments have unique sounds, but people are making music from random sounds by shaping and smoothing. Can you imagine the sounds you're hearing turned into notes? Can you change—by hearing selectively or more expansively—a larger pattern? Waves are easy; their pattern is incessant. If you're listening to traffic, can you discern the pulse of the green and red lights?

Now listen to all the sounds coming from speakers in a single room. Immerse yourself in that sound. Focus on it; make it louder. Loud enough to annoy you. Then focus away from it. Turn down the volume to a hum. Place all the sounds on a trailer—as if you could—and drive it away. Hear the sounds going down the block, fading into the distance.

Detach from your awareness. Detach from your hearing. Allow yourself to float away from the sounds without attachment without any reaction to them. Turn your attention inward to silence and try, if you can, not to hear anything at all.

Now we'll create an emotion we want to see beyond. We'll create a big bad emotion: an emotion that bothers you. As a caution, if this bothers you too much, don't do it. You don't have to. You can open your eyes and disengage and come back for the next exercise. This is just an exercise. Strength improves with repetition, but don't do too much.

Return to a calm, empty, and relaxed position, and imagine you are sitting in front of a big-screen TV. On this screen, conjure in your imagination the worst of all possible outcomes for your life. But before you do this, tell yourself that these are just ideas. You are creating negative thoughts in order to better control them. You will not nurture these thoughts, and you are not giving them soil in which to root. These are negative thoughts invited with intentions of peace, balance, and harmony.

I'm sure there are a host of possibilities, and I'm not asking you to go into detail. In fact, I'm not asking for any details at all. Simply get in touch with the feeling of deep despair that comes with what you most want to avoid. You have many choices and most likely, it's best to think of them in the abstract. I'm not even going to suggest possibilities because I want you to take full responsibility and have complete power to declaw them completely.

Focus on the feeling, not the causes, triggers, or events. Imagine your life is ending and you do not have, and maybe never had, those things most dear and meaningful to you. This is your depression in a test tube, a virus you hold with rubber gloves, searching for a vaccine. You must get to know this creature. It is not a predator, maybe not a parasite, maybe not even a destructive force in itself, but it is a vector of your defeat and despair. It, too, is one of God's children. What is it here for?

Step into the world of despair as if stepping into a hot reactor

Beyond Lucidity

wearing a radiation suit. A flimsy paper suit that only filters the air you breath. In 30 seconds your exposure will reach its limit, and you'll have to leave or be contaminated with the sickness. What can you do with your 30 seconds of despair? 30 seconds to parley with a force you fear to the bone. The opportunity is real but so is the risk.

If I've talked this exercise to a dull edge, you know how to sharpen it in an instant. I will not uncork the vial of your complete failure; I cannot accept responsibility. This may be an exercise you need to practice, not something to go full force on the first try. With every try you make, you'll have your time limit refreshed. It may even be extended. This is an art, not a science. You are tunneling into the caverns of emotion.

Turn once more to face the punctured eyes of your shriveled future. Some ghosts will consume you, others are starving for any life, and still others have a wisdom that will serve you. Until you meet them, you will not know to tell the difference. There are some lessons that can only be learned in hell. You would be well-served to find a guide. Before going too far, find yours.

Now step back from this critical reactor. I reel you back up with my safety line. I take you back outside and off the stage, out of the containment vessel, out of Hell's Gates. I am with you, and we look back on the scenes of your despair, a careful stage set, a frozen diorama, blazing in the spotlight of your attention, embedded in the black and trackless tunnel of the future.

I stand beside you while you cut the lights. There is a momentary fade as the hot filaments turn from white, to red, to glowing brown, and then all is dark. More than dark: gone. The image, the future, the ideas, and the emotions. All is black, without walls, or floor, or roof. Everything evaporates, boiling off like water in space, to leave nothing behind but the fluctuations of the vacuum.

It's your imagination. Scrooge's Ghost of Christmas Future. We all have this if we believe in opposites, a land inhabited by a better and a worse. It's not a reality; it is a tool. You may construct it, and use it, or find a path in which this never exists at all. Now it falls away. We have just The Void, both alive and lifeless. Home to nothing and crucible to all.

Let us sit in this empty space for a while. Let your thoughts drain away. Think about nothing as hard as you can. Stare deeply into the rich and textured darkness, the tabula rasa of all ideas.

Now for words. Fill your mind with words, a cacophony of verbiage. Open the gates of your mind's dictionary and let them spew out. There will be syllables and sentence fragments, interjections and exclamations. You can't think about it—that's too discerning—just babble as babies do, as you once did. It's the melody that counts, not the message. Scat singing, word salad. Consider this:

Perhaps it's a shrewd moment to take advantage of an open stance in shaping priorities with a naturally structured corollary to behavior change on the agenda of driving effective community toward reconciliation with future possibilities.

Or maybe it's the cat on a long run. Sunshine screaming its

disappearance that understands the land it works with. A man, a wall, a moon-line song. Door-walkers stealing cupcakes to run away posters singing. Gone to fling a rock, fly an ocean broomstick, quiet in the moon shine, starting with alarm.

Or could it be chronology, baby cursed rainfall, leasing grand puzzles growing fat. Alien vibrator gluttony evoking classic green weirdos with big heads. Blowtorch humble, orange flames gone to salty seamen waving from the poop deck down to us all. Topsy turvy, wall gone flippy, drowning in word salad until you forget. Just forget. Words, words, words.

Today's topics fade to grey onto a thin background of pleasant soundscapes. Oh, we think! Do we? I think so. Sometimes I might, but that's for later. Just hope for words to come out straight, whatever the meaning. I'll wait for time, sounds, and syllables. Clean the canvas; let's start over.

Now create a big wonderful emotion, one that attracts you. One that contains everything you have ever wanted. Love, support, confirmation, assurance, security, pleasure, rapture, ecstasy, and joy. This won't bother you… but maybe it should. People have overlooked many things when paradise is on offer—not everything that glitters is gold—yet panning for gold seems to be in our genes and if you don't look, you won't discover.

Return to a calm, empty, and relaxed position, and imagine the best of all possible outcomes for your life. You may be self-conscious, but don't hesitate here. Take out your laundry list of every possible great and wonderful thing you could ever hope for including those which, in your maturity and adulthood, you've outgrown and given up: true love and appreciation from your parents. Happiness throughout your family. The dissolution of all your self-doubts and the accomplishment of all your goals, your hopes, and dreams.

Take it beyond the hopeful, beyond the unlikely into the realm of the implausible, the incredible. Complete comfort and joyfulness. You have the foresight of knowing what will break before it happens: you just know. The full reward from all you invest in. An uncanny intuition for understanding people, the economy, the stock market. Experience the love of all your old pets. Telepathy, talking with animals, enlightenment. A sense of wonder, power, safety, and meaning.

These are your goals. If someone did them, why can't you? They will not occur unless you retain them, insist they're possible, and work toward each and every one. They come to some people in ones and twos. If you can live long enough, virtuously enough, with enough health, care, and wisdom they are yours to accomplish. You are limited first by what you believe are your limits. To deny those limits has the strange effect of placing you past them.

You would be shocked to realize just how many simple opportunities are left untaken simply due to a lack of confidence, curiosity, and whimsy. You would be astounded. We wander blind in a desert filled with diamonds… and all because we talk too much, listen too little, and fail to develop our subtle perception.

These may be just ideas, but they have power. You are creating positive thoughts to better control them. There is a bargain here, and it's an old story: there is a diamond on the summit, but you must climb the mountain.

You are not alone; you have support you have not met. You are attached, not just by need but obligation... to family, community, the collective. What you learn is taught to others. Your success blazes a trail others follow, many who are dear to you, and many more you've never met and never will.

With every advance you lift the species, and that's why the weight can feel so heavy. We want to be independent, but we need acceptance. It's a bargain. It's a trade. You borrow strength from what's around you, and you must return it. Like an astronaut lifted by technology, you serve those who lift you up. And you can, and you will do amazing things.

You are the apostle, preaching the possible, exhorting your eyes to open. These are powerful ideas. They have the promise to transform you. Let them root in the soil of your self-meaning. They are giddy, but they have consequences. You invite them with intentions of service, balance, and strength.

Now step back, out of the spotlight, off the stage, the dais, the clouds, the paradise. I am with you, and we look back on the scenes of your fulfillment, a careful stage set, a frozen diorama, blazing in the spotlight of your attention, embedded in the black and trackless tunnel of the future.

I stand beside you while you cut the lights. There is a momentary fade, as the hot filaments turn from white, to red, to glowing brown, and then all is dark. More than dark: gone. The

Becoming Lucid

image, the future, the ideas, and the emotions. All is black, without walls, or floor, or ceiling. Everything evaporates, boiling off like water in space, to leave nothing behind but the fluctuations of the vacuum.

What have you done? Compare your negative with your positive. Consider the benefit of visions and ideas. Where is the substance? In your mind? In the world? Anywhere at all?

What was more emotional? Was the negative stronger, more realistic, or artificial than the positive? Did one seem more "real"? Were you able to believe in what you were creating, or were you unwilling to flesh out all the feelings you stirred up?

You are built of different moods, attitudes, and inclinations. In you, there are different selves. Bring your normal, negative, and positive perspectives into conference, a three-way discussion as equals. Can you all be allies? Can you be a team?

Let's come back now, back to normal. To put back on the face that you've left in the jar by the door. I'll count down from five to one, and then we'll be finished here.

Five, resolve to make room for yourselves, all of yourselves. Each has their boundary, and it will take collaboration to move beyond these.

Four, each has a ladder to climb to their limit, but you'll find each ladder is too short.

Three, they are not too short when put together.

Two, above each of your senses of self is lucidity.

One, combining them is something even more.

Postscript

Once you reach a certain point, all fields of inquiry are asking the same questions. They're also stuck in the same paradigm and failing to progress because of that paradigm.

The failing paradigm is reductionism, which is being replaced by systems theory, emergent structures, phase transitions, and quantum mechanics. These ideas are just starting to pervade other fields. You may have heard of these things, but what you hear is largely misleading and wrong to the point of garbage. It's still too soon. If you want to learn these new concepts, study and teach them yourself.

These ideas are new. I have put some of them together here. I present the material in this book with little reference to mainstream sleep or dream research. Cutting edge work, some of which I bring to bear, has already jumped to these new paradigms. Surfing the crest of these new ideas yields a bountiful harvest.

Lincoln Stoller, 2019

For more information follow @LincolnStoller and #BecomingLucid, and visit my websites at:

www.mindstrengthbalance.com
and www.mindstrengthbooks.com.

THE END

References

Bear, Sun, Wabun Wind, and Shawnodese, *Dreaming With the Wheel: How to Interpret Your Dreams Using the Medicine Wheel.* New York, NY: Touchstone, 2012.

Bogzaran, Fariba, and Daniel Deslauriers, *Integral Dreaming, A Holistic Approach to Dreams.* Albany, NY: SUNY Press, 2012.

Campbell, Joseph, *Myths to Live By*, 2nd Edition. San Anselmo, CA : Joseph Campbell Foundation, 2011.

Hillman, James, *The Dream and the Underworld.* New York, NY: Harper and Row, 1979.

Johnson, Clare R., *Llewellyn's Complete Book of Lucid Dreaming, A Comprehensive Guide to Promote Creativity, Overcome Sleep Disturbances, and Enhance Health and Wellness.* Woodbury, MN: Llewellyn Publications, 2017.

Johnson, Robert, *Inner Work, Using Dreams and Active Imagination for Personal Growth.* New York, NY: HarperCollins, 1986.

Kunzendorf, R. G., and B. Wallace (Eds.), *Individual Differences in Conscious Experience.* Amsterdam: John Benjamins, 2000.

Molfese, Jerimiah, *My Adventures in Lucid Dreaming: A Dream Journal & Guide Into The World of Lucid Dreaming.* Bloomington, IN: AuthorHouse, 2012.

Taylor, Jeremy, *Where People Fly and Water Runs Uphill, Using Dreams to Tap the Wisdom of the Unconscious.* New

York, NY: Grand Central Publishing, 1993.

Walker, Matthew, *Why We Sleep, Unlocking the Power of Sleep and Dreams*. New York, NY: Simon and Schuster, 2017.

Windt, Jennifer M., Dreaming: *A Conceptual Framework for Philosophy of Mind and Empirical Research*. Cambridge, MA : MIT Press, 2017.

Zink, Nicolas and Reinhard Pietrowsky (2015). "Theories of Dreaming and Lucid Dreaming: An Integrative Review Towards Sleep, Dreaming, and Consciousness." *International Journal of Dream Research*, Vol. 8 (4), 35-53.

About the Author

Lincoln Stoller has published work as a physicist, astronomer, statistician, biologist, neurophysiologist, neurofeedback therapist, psychologist, hypnotherapist, computer scientist, software architect, anthropologist, mountaineer, and educator. He has designed and built two houses and has licenses to pilot soarplanes, fly paragliders, and scuba dive.

He holds a PhD in quantum physics from the University of Texas, hypnotherapy certifications from ICBCH and IMDHA, and the patent for the design of a business accounting system which he programmed, sold, and supported for 15 years. He is also an assessing editor at the *Journal of Mind and Behavior*.

Lincoln has spent 40 years involved with various schools of spirituality and mediation, 20 years with the therapeutic and religious use of psychedelics, 10 years designing and offering EEG brainwave training, and the last 5 years as a hypnotherapist in private practice specializing in medical support, sleep enhancement, spiritual guidance, and business psychology. His previous book, *The Learning Project, Rites of Passage*, explores the role of learning in how people live a meaningful life.

His 21-year-old son Kiran lives with Lincoln's ex-wife in New York, and his 8-year-old son Pythagoras lives with Lincoln in Victoria, British Columbia, Canada, to which he moved for educational and political reasons, and to be closer to mountains, forests, and the sea.

www.ingramcontent.com/pod-product-compliance
Lightning Source LLC
Chambersburg PA
CBHW020907080526
44589CB00011B/477